MENSA

MIGHTY MIND BENDERS

NEW
NUMBER
PUZZLES

If you have enjoyed the puzzles in this book why not try another title in the Mensa series?

Mensa New Word Puzzles
Mensa Logic Puzzles
Mensa Improve Your Mind Power
Mensa Family Quiz Book

THIS IS A CARLTON BOOK

Text and puzzle content copyright © British Mensa Limited 1997
Design and artwork copyright © Carlton Books Limited 1997

This edition published by Carlton Books Limited 1997

A CIP catalogue for this book is available from the British Library

ISBN 1-85868-250-9

Printed and bound in Italy

MENSA

MIGHTY MIND BENDERS

NEW
NUMBER
PUZZLES

John Bremner

CARLTON

CAN YOU JOIN MENSA?

Solving puzzles can be a rewarding experience. The moment when you discover you have unravelled the puzzle compiler's convoluted logic always brings a glow of satisfaction. But we thought you deserved something more. So Mensa are offering tangible proof of your mental prowess. Solve the following fiendish puzzles and we will send you a free certificate as proof of your achievement.

Puzzle 1

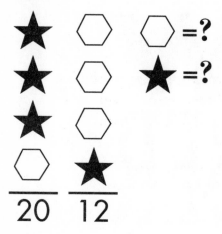

What are the missing values?

Puzzle 2

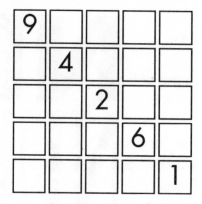

Using only the numbers already used, insert the numbers required to make all rows, columns and the remaining long diagonal add to 22.

Puzzle 3

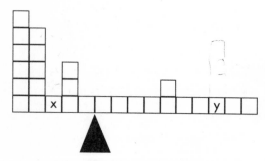

This system is in balance. If four additional blocks are placed above "x", how many need to be placed above "y" to return the system to balance?

Puzzle 4

20987152

Contained within the number above are two numbers which, when you multiply them together, produce **16777216** as a result. What are the two numbers to multiply?

• •

There, you did it! Now write the answers on a postcard, together with your name and address, and send them to Mensa Puzzle Challenge (Numbers), Mensa House, Freepost, Wolverhampton, WV2 1BR (no stamp needed). If your answers are correct we will send you a certificate and details of how to join Mensa.

INTRODUCTION

Number puzzles are perennially popular and such was the response to our last volume that it came as no surprise when the publisher demanded more. To bring a fresh feel to the project we have engaged a new author, John Bremner, whose skill at designing entertaining and stimulating puzzles is matched only by the boundless energy he brings to the task. John, I can confidently predict, will ensure that your mathematical skills are tested to the limit.

In this volume, as in many of the previous Mensa puzzle books, we have been fortunate in having the editorial services of David Ballheimer, himself a puzzler of awesome abilities. Our thanks to him for his many hours of checking and revising the proofs. Also we would like to thank our Series Editor, Liz Wheeler, and Series Art Editor, Paul Messam, who minister in a sort of guardian angel capacity over the entire series.

If you enjoy these puzzles you would enjoy Mensa. There you can meet people from all walks of life but of similar brain power. Mensa is quite simply a wonderful social club which spans the world and allows people with intellectual interests to get together for their mutual benefit and entertainment. There are 120,000 Mensans throughout the world, so why not join us? Details can be obtained from: Mensa House, St John's Square, Wolverhampton, WV2 4AH England (tel 01902 772771). American Mensa Limited is at 2626 E14th Street, Brooklyn, New York 11235-3992, USA, or contact Mensa International, 15 The Ivories, 628 Northampton Street, London N1 2NY, England who will be happy to put you in touch with your own national Mensa.

R. P. Allen

Robert Allen
Editorial Director
Mensa Publications

Insert the missing numbers. In each pattern the missing number has something to do with the surrounding numbers in combination.

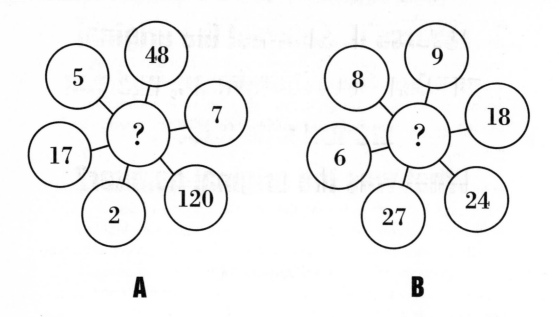

A

B

SEE ANSWER 44

If Picasso is worth 28 and Monet is worth 22, how much is Raphael worth?

SEE ANSWER 83

Take a five-digit number and reverse it. Subtract the original number from its reverse, and you are left with 33957. What was the original number?

SEE ANSWER 35

PUZZLE 4

What number should replace the question mark?

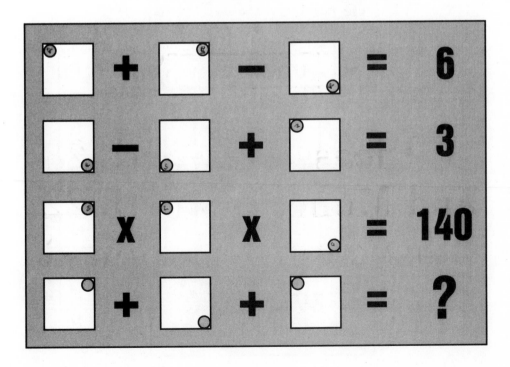

SEE ANSWER 50

Za-za is older than Fifi, but younger than Juan. Fifi is older than Jorjio and Maccio. Maccio is younger than both Carlos and Jorjio. Juan is older than both Fifi and Maccio, but younger than Carlos. Who is the oldest, and who is the youngest?

SEE ANSWER 61

PUZZLE 6

When the shaded sections of this puzzle are brought together, one of the white patches is inserted into the middle to make a magic square in which all rows, columns and long diagonals add to 49. Is it patch A, B, C or D?

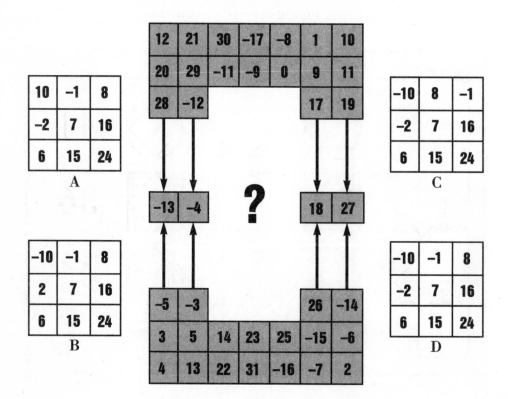

SEE ANSWER 75

A rectangular swimming pool of constant depth is twice as long as it is wide, but the owner is unhappy with the dimensions of the pool. The length is reduced by 12 units and its width increased by 10 units. When this is done, the modified pool will hold exactly the same volume of water. What were the pool's original dimensions?

SEE ANSWER 23

PUZZLE 8

Each shape is made up of two items, and each same shape has the same value, whether in the foreground or background. What number should replace the question mark?

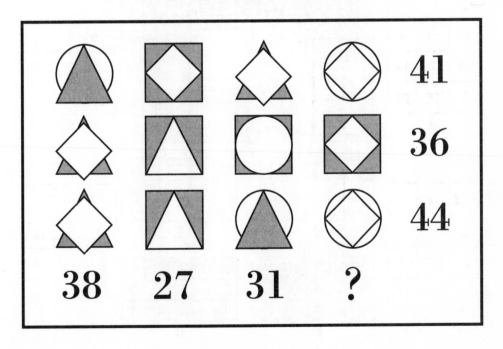

SEE ANSWER 33

9

What is the area of the shaded path, if the path is one unit wide?

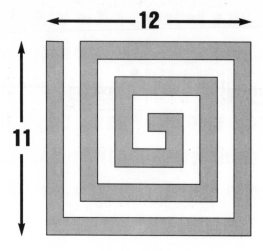

SEE ANSWER 46

PUZZLE 10

The panel below, when complete, contains the binary numbers from 1 to 25. Does binary patch A, B, C or D complete the panel?

SEE ANSWER 17

Which letters, based on the alphanumeric system,
should go into the blank boxes?

6	1	7	3
1	3	5	4
7	7	0	9

A H B

5	1	3	9
2	8	6	4
8	6	2	6

F B C

2	2	9	2
4	3	0	9
7	1	7	8

SEE ANSWER 55

PUZZLE 12

What number, when you multiply it by 5 and add 6, then multiply that result by 4 and add 9, gives you a number that, when you multiply it by 5 and subtract 165, gives you a number that, when you knock off the last 2 digits, brings you back to your original number?

SEE ANSWER 84

What number should replace the question mark?

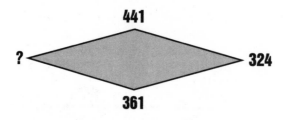

SEE ANSWER 76

PUZZLE 14

If each large ball weighs one and a third times the weight of each little ball, what is the minimum number of balls that need to be added to the right-hand side to make the scales balance?

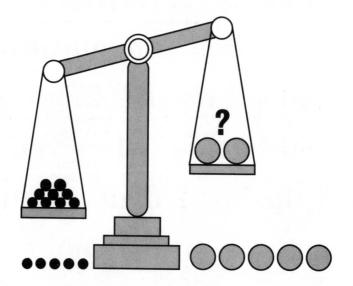

SEE ANSWER 6

Present at Juan's birthday party were a father-in-law, a
mother-in-law, a daughter-in-law, two sons, two daughters, two
sisters and a brother, four children, three grandchildren, two
fathers, two mothers, a grandfather, and a grandmother.
However, family relationships can be complicated.
One man's brother can, of course, be another man's
brother-in-law, and at the same time, someone's son.
With that in mind, what is the smallest number of people
needed at the party for the above relationships to exist?

SEE ANSWER 27

PUZZLE 16

How many rosettes are missing from the blank circle?

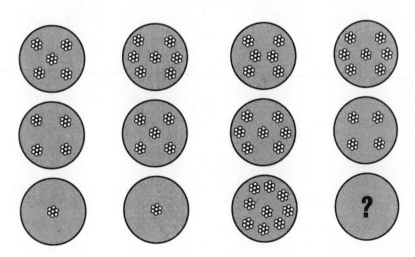

SEE ANSWER 85

Forty people took part in a freestyle race. Twenty people ran. Ten people dashed. Five people bolted and sprinted. Three people bolted, dashed, ran and sprinted. Two people ran, bolted, and sprinted. Five people ran and sprinted. Two people dashed, ran, and sprinted. How many people neither dashed, ran, bolted, nor sprinted?

SEE ANSWER 69

What value needs to go into the upper box to bring this system into balance? Note: The beam is broken down into equal parts and the value of each box is taken from its midpoint.

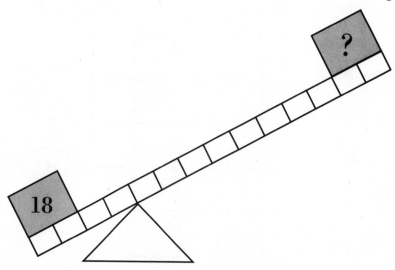

SEE ANSWER 41

PUZZLE 19

Find a route from the top of this puzzle to the bottom that arrives at the total 353, always going down and to an adjoining hexagon.

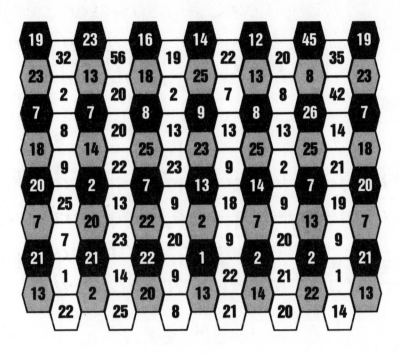

SEE ANSWER 15

PUZZLE 20

Using only the numbers already used, complete this puzzle to make all the rows, columns, and long diagonals add to 27.

6				
			2	
	9			
				3
		7		

SEE ANSWER 21

PUZZLE 21

Insert the supplied rows of numbers into the appropriate places in the grid to make all rows, columns and long diagonals add to 17.
Example: (C) goes into the location (a).

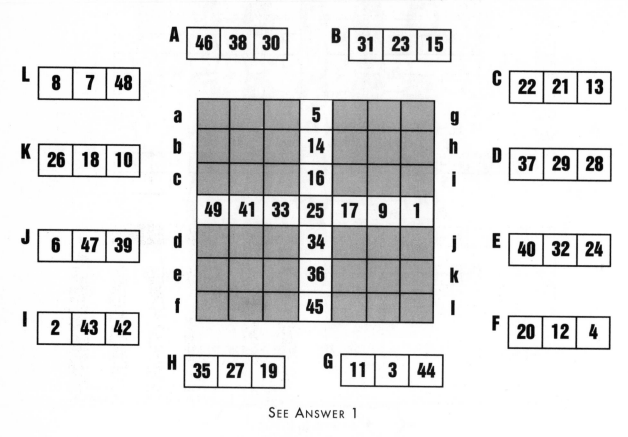

A | 46 | 38 | 30   **B** | 31 | 23 | 15

L | 8 | 7 | 48   **C** | 22 | 21 | 13

K | 26 | 18 | 10   **D** | 37 | 29 | 28

J | 6 | 47 | 39   **E** | 40 | 32 | 24

I | 2 | 43 | 42   **F** | 20 | 12 | 4

H | 35 | 27 | 19   **G** | 11 | 3 | 44

SEE ANSWER 1

PUZZLE 22

At 3pm one day, a flagpole and a measuring pole cast shadows as shown. What length is the flagpole?

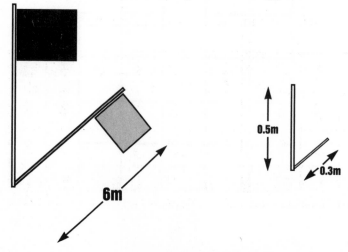

6m

0.5m

0.3m

SEE ANSWER 34

Use logic to discover which shape has the greatest perimeter.

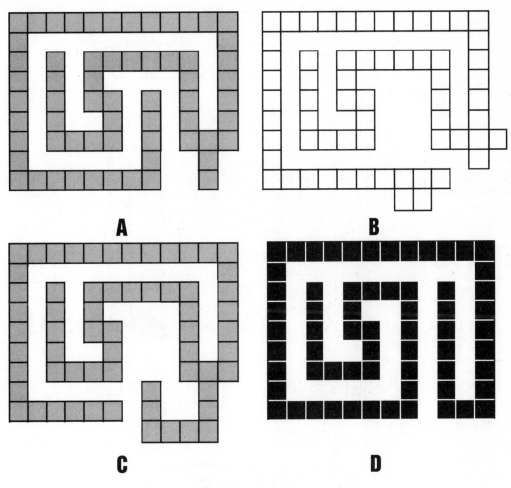

A   B

C   D

SEE ANSWER 49

PUZZLE 24

Crack the code to find the missing number.

A	B	C	D	E	F	G	H	I	J
9	3	8	7	8	9	2	8	5	7
1	2	1	5	?	7	1	0	1	2
K	L	M	N	O	P	Q	R	S	T

SEE ANSWER 70

What number should replace the question mark?

6   8   4   8   7   9   6   ?

SEE ANSWER 36

PUZZLE 26

Which number replaces the question mark?
What is the value of each animal?

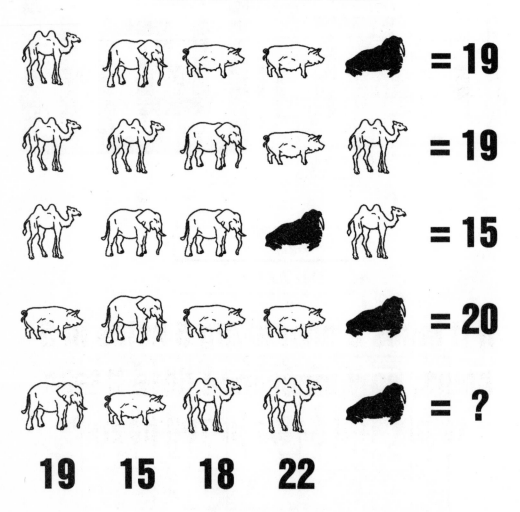

19   15   18   22

SEE ANSWER 13

PUZZLE 27

What number should replace the question mark?

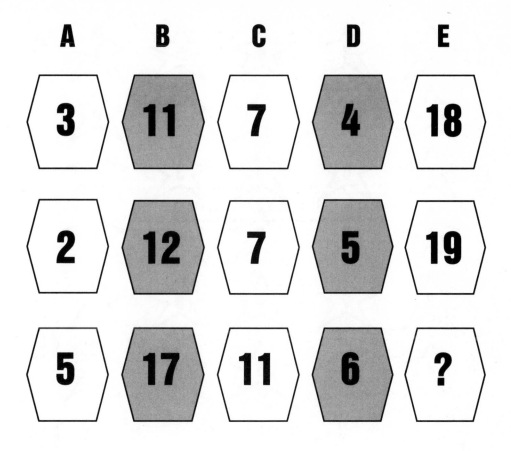

SEE ANSWER 32

PUZZLE 28

If it takes 5 men to dig 5 holes in 5 hours, how many men does it take to dig 100 holes in 100 hours?

SEE ANSWER 72

PUZZLE 29

Put the right number in the blank star.

SEE ANSWER 22

PUZZLE 30

If you buy 9 barrels of beer for 25 Credits each, but you are given a 25% discount on the last 4 barrels, and you are given in change 3 times the cost of all the barrels less half the value that your discount would be if your discount were 25% more for the last 2 barrels than the discount you were actually given, what was the total cost of the barrels ?

SEE ANSWER 9

Starting from any square on the top row, you can accumulate points by stepping down diagonally to another, adjoining square, and adding that to your total. You may not land on a square containing the number one, or on any square horizontally adjacent to a square with a one, but you may start from such a square.

You may not travel up or sideways. By continuing this process until you reach a square on the bottom row, what is the maximum number of points it is possible to accumulate?

9	4	5	3	6	1	8	2
8	1	2	2	3	2	5	1
6	9	9	1	2	4	3	5
4	8	1	3	5	2	6	1
1	4	3	7	6	3	1	4
9	2	4	8	6	4	5	3
4	2	9	4	8	6	7	1
2	8	1	6	5	9	0	1

SEE ANSWER 37

When a ball is dropped from a height of 9 m, it bounces back two-thirds of the way. Assuming that the ball comes to rest after making a bounce which takes it less than 2 mm high, how many times does it bounce?

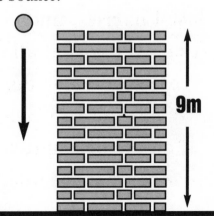

9m

SEE ANSWER 66

The planet Pento is inhabited by a race of highly intelligent one-toed quadrupeds with elephant-like trunks. So with four toes and a trunk, they have adopted the five base for their number system. With that in mind, convert the Pento number 1234 into its decimal equivalent.

SEE ANSWER 42

PUZZLE 34

Which number should replace the question mark?

SEE ANSWER 28

PUZZLE 35

These systems are in balance. What weight is required in
the right hand box to balance the load ?

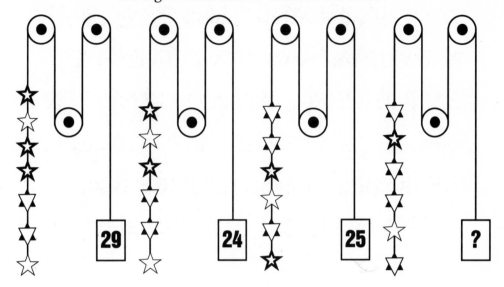

SEE ANSWER 54

PUZZLE 36

Each same shape has the same value. What number should
replace the question mark

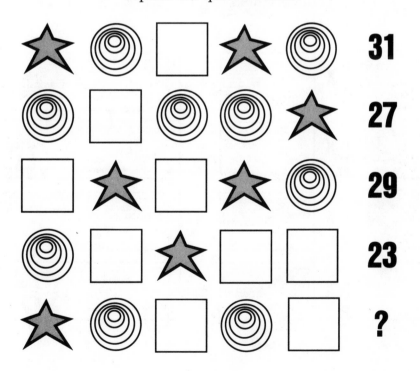

SEE ANSWER 82

23

Find the missing number.

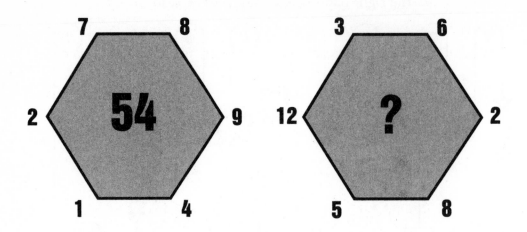

SEE ANSWER 8

PUZZLE 38

What three-digit number should replace the question mark?

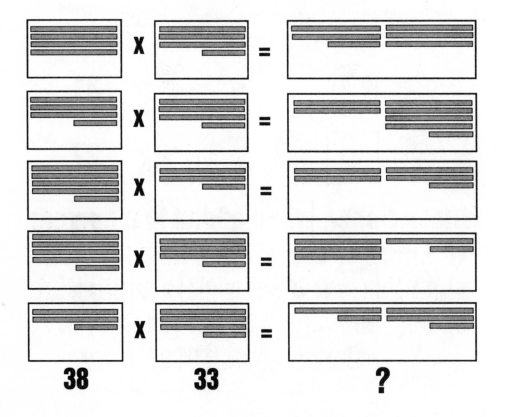

38   **33**   **?**

SEE ANSWER 77

The three balls at the top of each hexagon should contain numbers that, when added together and subtracted from the total of the numbers in the three balls at the bottom of each hexagon, equal the number inside each relevant hexagon. Insert the missing numbers.

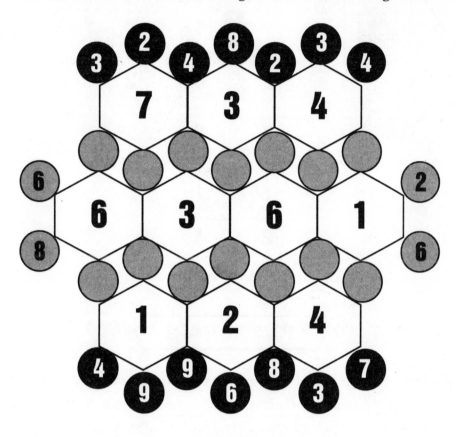

SEE ANSWER 58

What number, when added to a number 10 times as big, gives a number that, when its right-hand digit is multiplied by four and added to the result of the above, gives 1000?

SEE ANSWER 12

What number should replace the question mark?

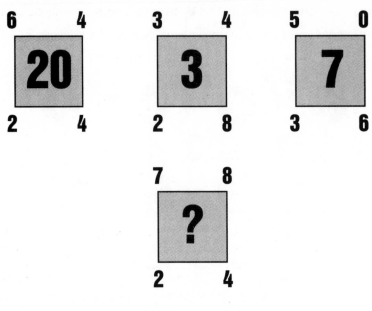

SEE ANSWER 38

PUZZLE 42

This clock has been designed for a planet that rotates on its axis once every 16 hours. There are 64 minutes to every hour, and 64 seconds to the minute. At the moment, the time on the clock reads a quarter to eight. What time, to the nearest second, will the clock say the time after the next time the hands appear to meet?

SEE ANSWER 25

PUZZLE 43

A large sheet of paper is 0.1 mm thick. A man amuses
himself by tearing it in half and putting both pieces together,
and then tearing those into four sheets, and repeating the
process until he has done it twenty-five times.
How high is the stack of paper now?

a) As thick as a book   b) As high as a man   c) As high as a house
d) As high as a mountain

SEE ANSWER 29

PUZZLE 44

This is a time puzzle. Which symbol is missing?
Is it A, B, C, D, E or F?

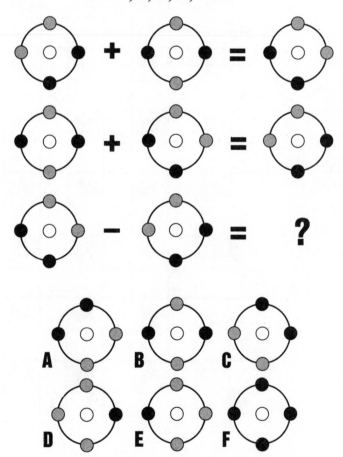

SEE ANSWER 81

27

Which number should replace the question mark?

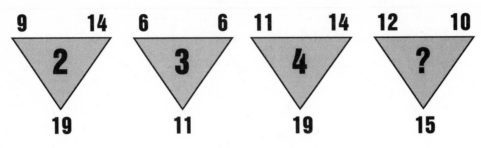

SEE ANSWER 16

PUZZLE 46

Insert in the boxes at the corner of each shaded number-square, the digits which are multiplied together to give the numbers in the shaded boxes. For example, in the bottom left corner, 144 is derived from 3 x 6 x 8 (and another multiplier – here 1), but you also have to consider how this helps to make solutions for the surrounding numbers... and so on.

3		5		4		4		3		3
	90		120		64		144		54	
2										1
	48		96		16		72		36	
1										2
	160		80		20		150		30	
4										1
	180		10		40		100		15	
9										3
	27		8		32		12		81	
3										9
	24		28		84		45		135	
8										1
	144		42		63		225		25	
3		6		1		3		5		1

SEE ANSWER 64

What number should replace the question mark?

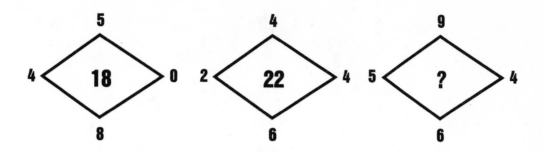

SEE ANSWER 40

Each like symbol has the same value. Supply the missing total.

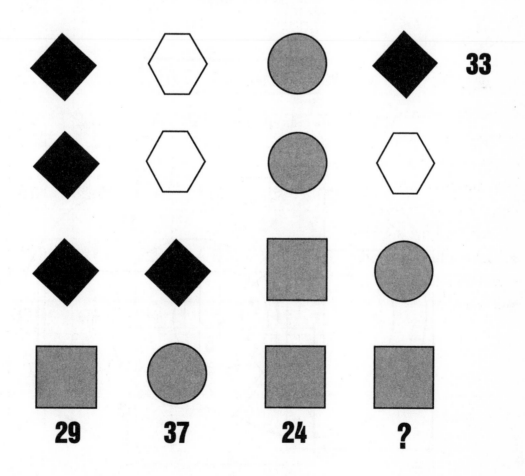

33

29   37   24   ?

SEE ANSWER 3

PUZZLE 49

What time will it be, to the nearest second, when the hands of this clock next appear to meet?

SEE ANSWER 11

PUZZLE 50

What number should replace the question mark?

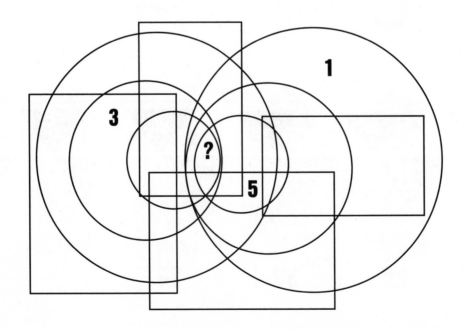

1

3

?

5

SEE ANSWER 31

Insert the missing numbers in the blank hexagons.

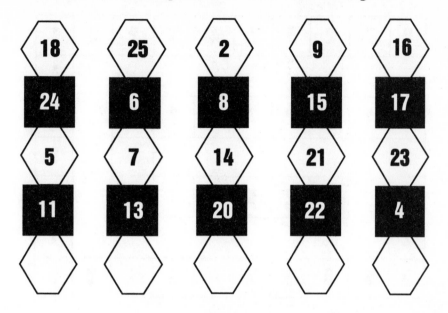

SEE ANSWER 62

What number should replace the question mark?

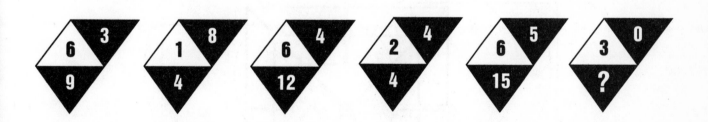

SEE ANSWER 56

What number should replace the question mark?

9	7	2	5	7	4	3	2	5	1
									4
9	4	5	2	7	5	2	7		5
3							9		9
6		?	2	6	5	1	8		8
2									1
8	3	5	2	7	4	3	3	6	5

SEE ANSWER 73

PUZZLE 54

Black counters are nominally worth 4.
White counters are nominally worth 3.
Being on a diagonal trebles a counter's value.
Being on the innermost box doubles a counter's value.
Being on the outermost box halves a counter's value.
The rules work in combination.
What is the total value of all the counters on the board?

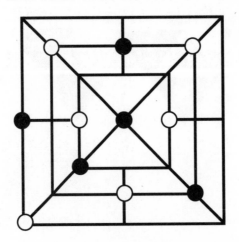

SEE ANSWER 43

What number continues the sequence?

15   20   20   6   6   ?

SEE ANSWER 20

PUZZLE 56

I have a deck of cards from which some
are missing. If I deal them equally
between nine people, I have two cards
to spare. If I deal them equally between
four people, I have three cards to spare.
If I deal them between seven people,
I have five cards to spare. There
are normally 52 cards in the deck.

How many are missing?

SEE ANSWER 47

Each same symbol has the same value. What number should replace
the question mark?

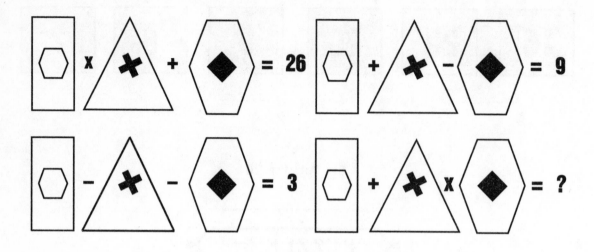

SEE ANSWER 74

PUZZLE 58

What number should replace the question mark?

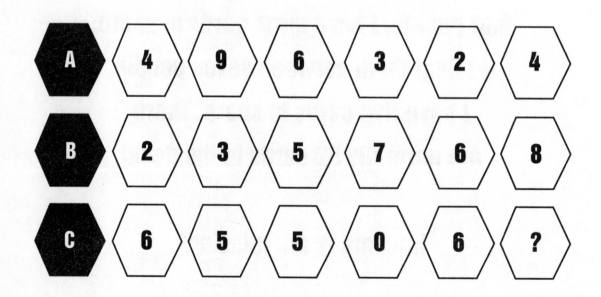

SEE ANSWER 53

PUZZLE 59

What number should replace the question mark in the blank square?

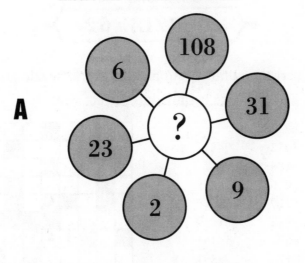

SEE ANSWER 19

PUZZLE 60

Insert the central numbers.

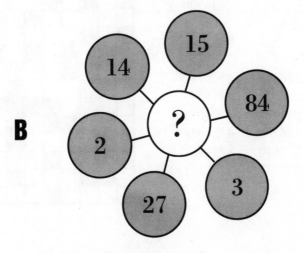

SEE ANSWER 4

The load on this beam and rollers apparatus has to be moved a distance of 20 units. If the circumference of each of the rollers is 0.8 units, how many turns must the rollers make to accomplish the move?

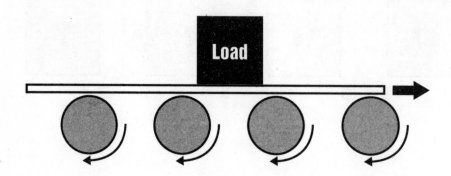

SEE ANSWER 45

PUZZLE 62

Insert the numbers supplied into the puzzle grid.
There is only one correct way.

ACROSS

118	916	3052	9481
155	951	3184	9857
200	0193	5056	16659
277	0360	5119	35677
293	1048	5832	51719
390	1066	6073	56151
653	1918	7176	76891
724	2390	7775	6036300
915	2983	8885	7424361

DOWN

08	5667	72612	897511
49	7900	87333	965853
63	8659	95138	3704058
66	8890	116765	4756628
69	10875	215810	6754451
90	50713	353637	229137152
4920	62817	675856	248143773
5086			

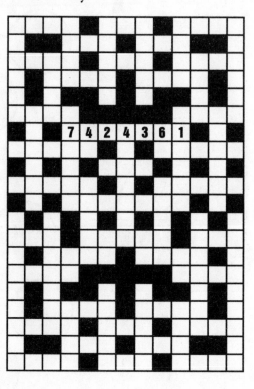

SEE ANSWER 57

PUZZLE 63

What number should replace the question mark?

SEE ANSWER 48

PUZZLE 64

The symbols represent the numbers 1 to 9.
Work out the value of the missing multiplier.

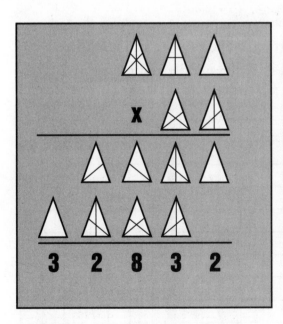

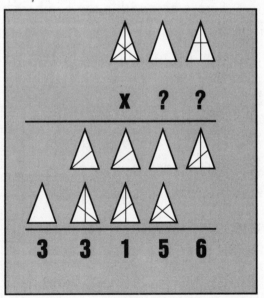

SEE ANSWER 51

This system is balanced. How heavy is the black box (ignoring leverage effects)?

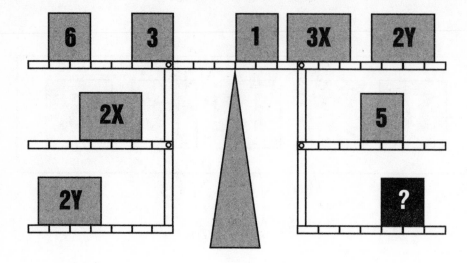

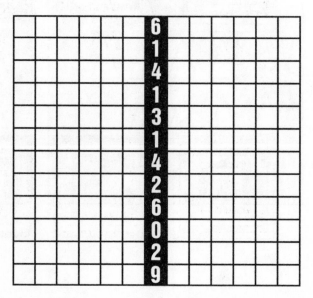

SEE ANSWER 86

PUZZLE 66

Somewhere within the numbers below left, there is a number that, if it is put into the grid below, starting at the top left and working from left to right, row by row, will have the middle column as shown when the grid is completed. Put in the missing numbers.

3095867235697809123948566
8094164162223456341219183
6216144432708929846152955
0016219320002528131215858
7193945046395123161762113
2677922896561231022384046
1289854043261614252616093
4172858300912428596481342
5683099801284730613339021

SEE ANSWER 60

$$2 \times \sqrt{2} = \sqrt{8}$$

$$3 \times \sqrt{5} = \sqrt{45}$$

What number should replace the question mark?

$$4 \times \sqrt{6} = \sqrt{?}$$

SEE ANSWER 2

PUZZLE 68

The black, white and shaded rings of this square target always have the same value, irrespective of their position, and each target is worth 44. Which of the targets, A, B, C or D, will replace the question mark?

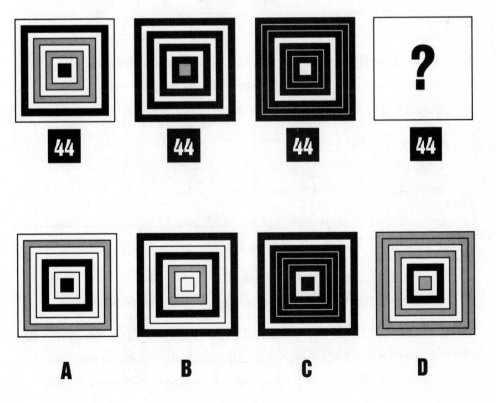

SEE ANSWER 30

How many different ways is it possible to arrange the order of these four kings?

SEE ANSWER 65

⟨ **PUZZLE 70** ⟩

Find this famous historical date.

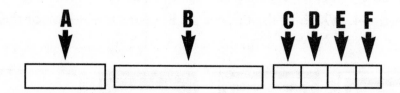

A. The two digit number that, when you divide it by two and add one, then square the result, gives a number that when you subtract one and divide it by ten, gives you twelve.

B. The month that comes three months after the month that comes seven months before the month that is a month before the month that comes nine months after March.

C. The number that, when you square it, add the result to itself, and multiply the result of that by ten, gives you the date in A.

D. The number that, when you square it and add both of the resulting digits together, brings back your original number.

E. The number that, when you add four and multiply the result by ten, gives a number that when added to the original number plus two, and divided by four, gives twenty-seven as a result.

SEE ANSWER 18

If the top left intersection is worth 1, and the bottom right
intersection is worth 25, which of these nodule grids,
A, B, C or D, is worth 67?

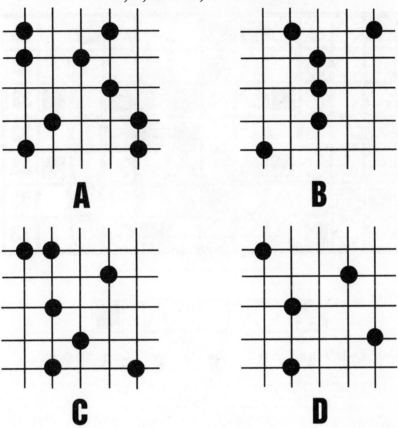

A   **B**

C   **D**

SEE ANSWER 79

PUZZLE 72

Previous to the time shown, when were all four
of the digits on this watch last on display?

SEE ANSWER 67

Each like shape has the same value. Which is the missing symbol?

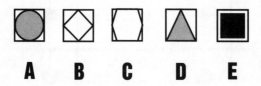

A   B   C   D   E

SEE ANSWER 26

┌──────────────────┐
│   PUZZLE 74   │
└──────────────────┘

Find within the number below, two numbers, one of which is double the other, and which when added together make 10743.

5716 2383581

SEE ANSWER 14

PUZZLE 75

This system is balance. How heavy is the black weight
(ignoring leverage effects)?

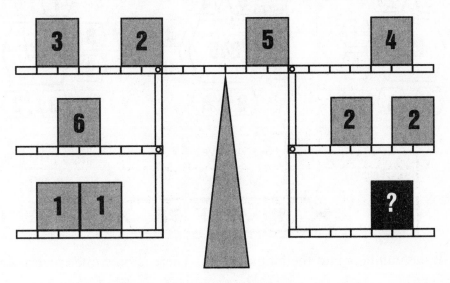

SEE ANSWER 24

PUZZLE 76

There are logical differences in the way each of these squares
work, but they all involve simple addition or subtraction of rows.
What are the missing numbers?

A

2	6	3	0	8	a
3	8	0	3	9	b
2	3	?	5	7	c
1	9	2	5	4	d
2	1	5	3	6	e

B

2	1	3	2	0	a
1	3	5	6	2	b
0	5	?	4	7	c
2	9	6	3	0	d
1	0	2	9	9	e

C

3	1	2	0	9	a
6	1	4	6	2	b
2	8	?	1	9	c
4	9	6	5	7	d
7	1	3	3	3	e

D

3	3	6	4	7	a
3	3	6	1	1	b
1	1	?	2	0	c
3	4	1	0	6	d
2	1	9	3	2	e

SEE ANSWER 71

PUZZLE 77

What number should replace the question
mark in the third hexagon pattern?

SEE ANSWER 59

PUZZLE 78

Fill the numbers into the blank spaces. There is only one correct way.

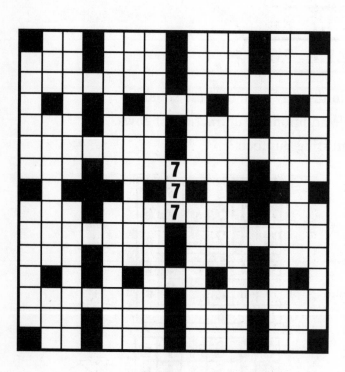

ACROSS

29	345	477	1052151
47	389	485	1285465
58	394	488	1469451
81	409	510	1779317
012	416	550	2008732
018	437	563	2457149
048	439	746	2857375
142	448	775	5125721
192	459	819	5418409
314	473	907	9588859

DOWN

138	777	1949159	6656485
198	158453	2193241	7413313
231	219952	2443740	8475941
250	420417	3854345	8614451
410	590579	4112340	8724315
473	0474542	5984178	9855707
745	1274458	6584404	9905865
750			

SEE ANSWER 7

PUZZLE 79

The squares of the times it takes planets to go round their sun are proportional to the cubes of the major axes of their orbits. With this in mind, if CD is four times AB, and a year on the planet Zero lasts for six earth years, how long is a year on the planet Hot?

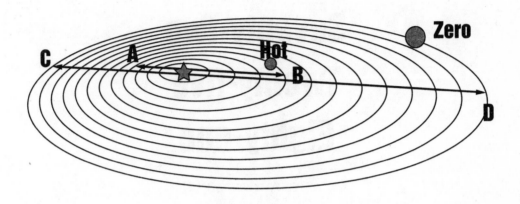

SEE ANSWER 68

PUZZLE 80

Put the stars into the boxes in such a way that each row is double the row below.

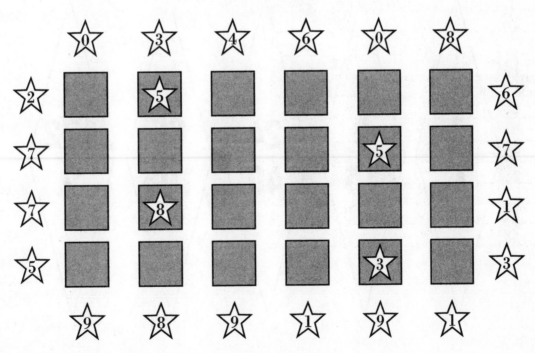

SEE ANSWER 10

Which is the odd number out?

Thirty-six
Sixty-four
Seventy-two
Twenty-five
Eighty-one

SEE ANSWER 63

What number should replace the question mark?

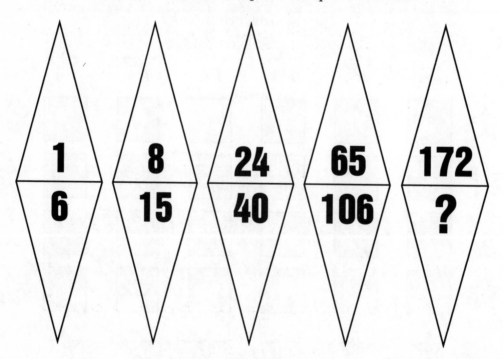

SEE ANSWER 80

Insert the missing numbers to make each row, column,
and long diagonal add to 189.

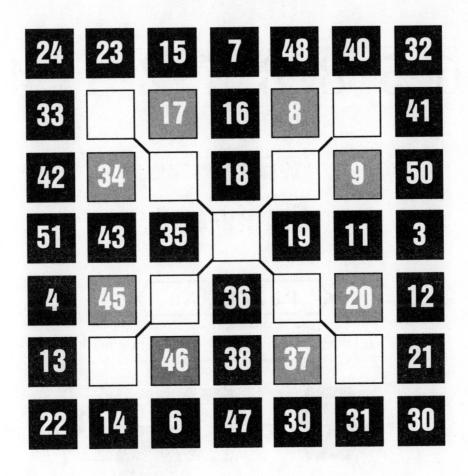

SEE ANSWER 52

PUZZLE 84

In 1952, New Year's Day was on a Tuesday. What day of the week was New Year's Day in 1953?

SEE ANSWER 5

PUZZLE 85

Find two numbers, contained within the number below,
which give 8647492 when multiplied together.

6 5 8 8 7 2 1 4

SEE ANSWER 78

PUZZLE 86

What number should replace the question mark?

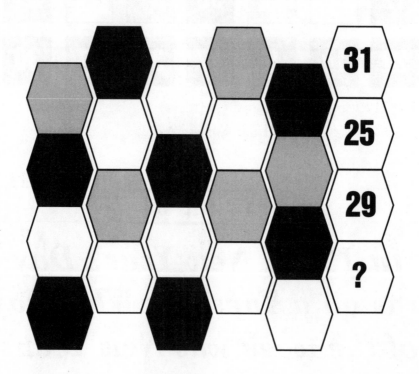

SEE ANSWER 39

What is the missing number?

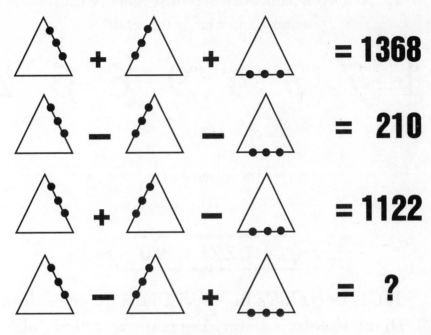

= 1368

= 210

= 1122

= ?

SEE ANSWER 121

PUZZLE 88

Five of these numbers interact together to give the number 1 as a solution. Which five numbers, and in which order?

+ 19	x 9	+ 29	x 7	- 999
- 94	+ 173	+ 65	- 236	x 8
+ 122	x 5	x 212	+ 577	- 567
+ 190	x 6	x 4	- 435	x 22
x 13	- 87	x 12	- 172	+ 117

SEE ANSWER 182

The number below, when the digits are rearranged and multiplied by 63, produces a particularly repetitive result. What is the new number and what is the result?

1 7 3 4 9 6 5 2

SEE ANSWER 110

Jon is Lorraine's brother. Diane married Jon. Diane is John's sister. Lorraine married John. Diane and Jon had seven grandchildren. Diane and Jon had three children. Lorraine and John had two children. Lorraine and John had seven grandchildren. Ricardo, one of Diane and Jon's children, and a cousin to Lorna-Jane and Frazier, did not marry, and had no offspring. Diane and Jon had two other children – Juan and Suzi. Lorraine and John had two children – Lorna-Jane and Frazier. Lorna-Jane married Juan, and had four children. Frazier married Suzi and had three children. Lorraine and John had twins. Frazier and Juan were cousins. Suzi and Lorna-Jane were cousins. Ricardo had a sister. Lorna-Jane had a brother. Frazier had a sister. Suzi had two brothers. For the above relationships to exist, how many were there, grandparents, parents, children, cousins and siblings in all?

SEE ANSWER 138

Map the alphabet into two rows to work out the value
of N and hence P.

| F = 25 | O = 17 | L = 37 | P = N + 4 |

SEE ANSWER 87

PUZZLE 92

Decode the logic of the puzzle to find the missing number.

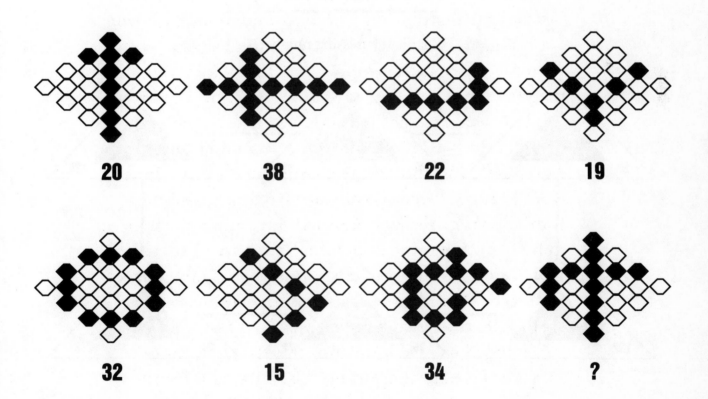

20   38   22   19

32   15   34   ?

SEE ANSWER 103

Insert the columns into the appropriate places to make both long diagonals add to 182. The middle column, (D), has been done for you.

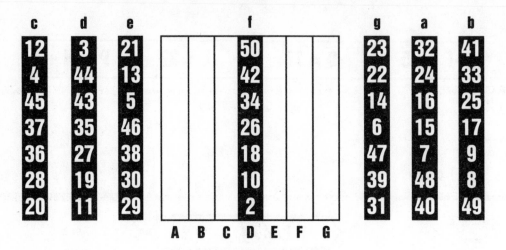

SEE ANSWER 134

PUZZLE 94

What is the missing number?

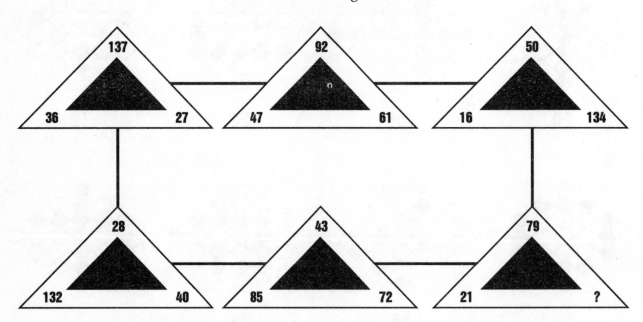

These systems are in balance. What is the missing number?

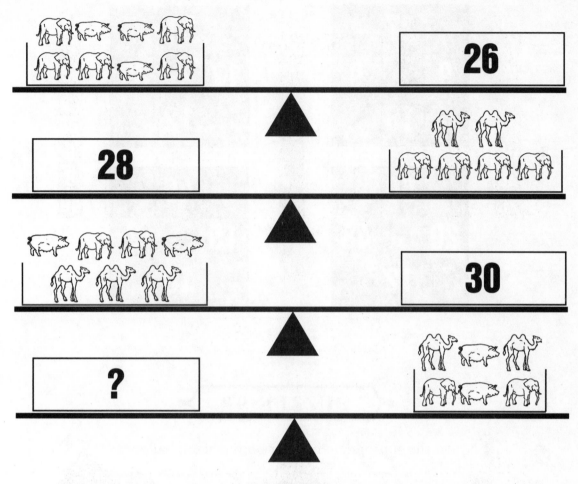

SEE ANSWER 159

PUZZLE 96

Find this 6-digit number.
First 3 digits – last 3 digits = 665. Within the number there is a 3 to the left of a 1. There is a 0. There is a 7 to the right of a 9. There is a 5 to the left of a 3.

SEE ANSWER 104

PUZZLE 97

What is the missing number?

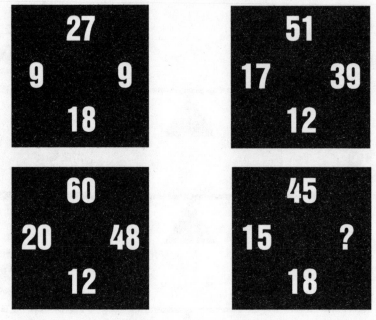

SEE ANSWER 160

PUZZLE 98

Put the appropriate number on the blank balloon.

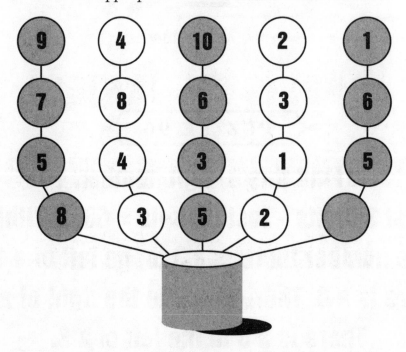

SEE ANSWER 167

Fill in the blanks for Espresso.

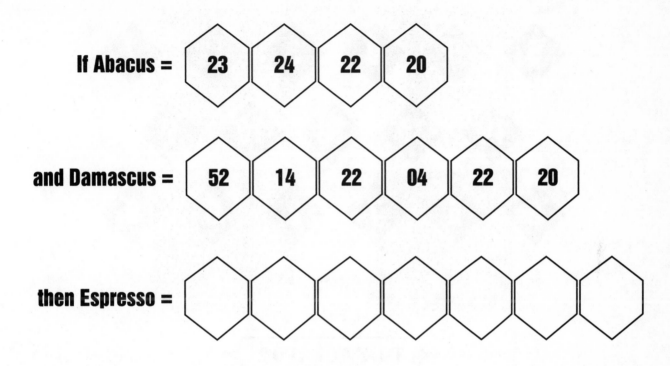

If Abacus = 23 24 22 20

and Damascus = 52 14 22 04 22 20

then Espresso =

SEE ANSWER 156

PUZZLE 100

What is the largest number you can write with three digits?

SEE ANSWER 122

PUZZLE 101

What is the missing number?

SEE ANSWER 183

PUZZLE 102

What is the missing number?

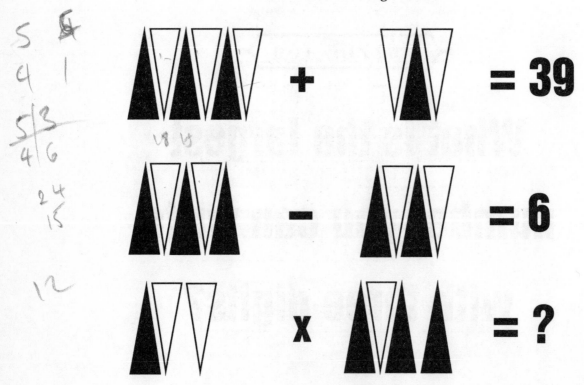

SEE ANSWER 111

PUZZLE 103

What 6-figure number, found within 3691428570, when multiplied by every number between 1 and 6, results in a number with the same digits rearranged each time?

SEE ANSWER 139

PUZZLE 104

Which of the supplied tiles, A, B, C, D, E or F, logically fits into the vacant space?

A
8	8	2
2	9	2
4	7	1

B
2	8	2
1	8	1
4	7	2

C
2	8	2
1	8	1
4	7	1

2	9	3	7	3	2	1	1	8	
		5	4	3	8	4	2	4	2	0
8	3	5	6	6	3	0	2	4	
		7	2	9	2	4	1	8	1	4
6	4	7	4	4	2	8	2	4	
		7	2				1	6	1	4
6	2	9	2	6	**?**	2		
		3	9				2	8	2	7
3	4	5	4	8	2	0	1	2	
		2	8	6	3	2	1	8	1	6
2	9	4	6	6	2	4	1	8	
		7	6	8	6	6	4	8	4	2
5	5	9	3	2	2	7	2	5	

D
2	8	2
2	9	2
4	7	1

E
2	8	2
1	9	1
4	5	1

F
3	8	3
1	8	1
4	7	1

SEE ANSWER 88

PUZZLE 105

Five armadillos = two pigs

One pig + one cat = one dog

One armadillo + one cat = one horse

Four pigs + two armadillos = two dogs

Four horses + three dogs = five cats + seven pigs + one armadillo

If armadillos are worth 2, what are the values of the
dogs, horses, cats and pigs?

SEE ANSWER 155

PUZZLE 106

In the blank hexagon at the corner of each black box, write a
single-digit number which, when added to the other three corner
numbers, equals the total in the middle. For example, 25 could be
5 + 5 + 6 + 9. But you have to consider how the surrounding totals,
20, 19, and 21, will be affected by your choice. You must use each
number – including 0 – at least once.

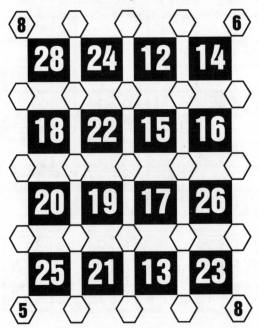

SEE ANSWER 135

PUZZLE 107

What is the missing number?

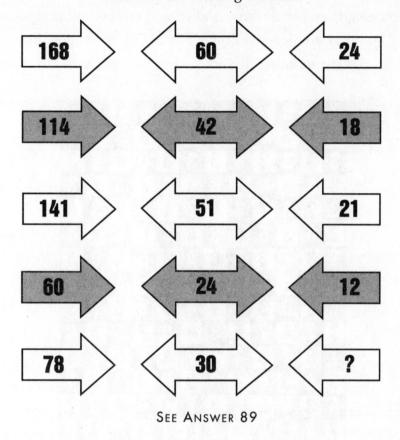

SEE ANSWER 89

PUZZLE 108

Put the appropriate number in the blank triangle.

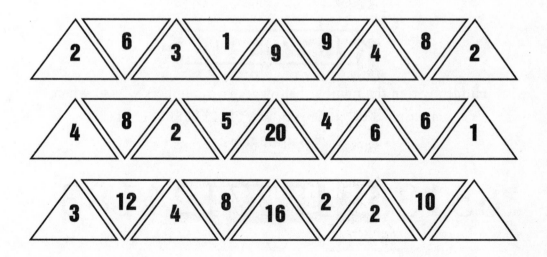

SEE ANSWER 105

Find the continuous sequence of 76384 in the grid below,
starting from the top row and ending on the bottom row.
You may go along or down, but not up or diagonally.
The numbers are not all in a straight line.

7	7	8	7	8	7	3	7	6	3	8	7
6	6	6	4	6	7	6	3	3	4	6
3	3	3	3	8	3	3	3	8	4	8	3
8	4	8	4	7	8	3	8	6	4	7	8
3	7	3	7	3	4	7	4	7	7	3	4
3	6	3	6	8	3	4	3	6	3	8	4
7	3	7	3	3	8	4	8	6	8	8	4
7	8	7	8	4	8	7	6	7	4	3	8
8	3	8	3	7	4	3	3	6	7	3
3	7	4	7	6	3	4	8	7	3	3	4
7	8	7	8	3	3	7	4	7	6	3	4
3	4	3	4	7	3	8	3	8	7	8	4
4	3	4	3	6	7	7	3	4	8	3	7
7	4	7	4	4	3	4	3	8	3	8	6
8	3	8	3	3	7	4	3	8	4	4	7

SEE ANSWER 136

Hidden within the number below are two numbers which, when
multiplied together, produce 1111111111111111.
What are they?

6513594777124183

SEE ANSWER 161

Complete the analogy.

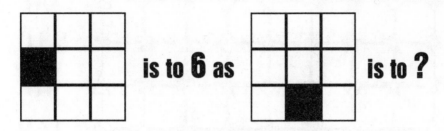

SEE ANSWER 123

PUZZLE 112

Fill the numbers into the blank spaces. There is only one correct way.

ACROSS

118	2133	6289
126	2345	6321
149	2801	9134
197	2803	9277
421	3458	9783
738	3482	12304
769	3485	12334
823	4190	12345
864	4227	53802
932	4656	56182
987	5199	0693878
1366	5660	9124914

DOWN

14	8228	443628
15	9998	492660
25	12735	536293
33	15787	593680
39	17151	4143383
42	24991	5428292
1178	26114	6132104
2119	64843	586713226
3002	116357	981921603
6334	200900	

SEE ANSWER 147

The only symbols that concern you in this multiplication puzzle are stars. Using their positions on the grid, calculate the missing number.

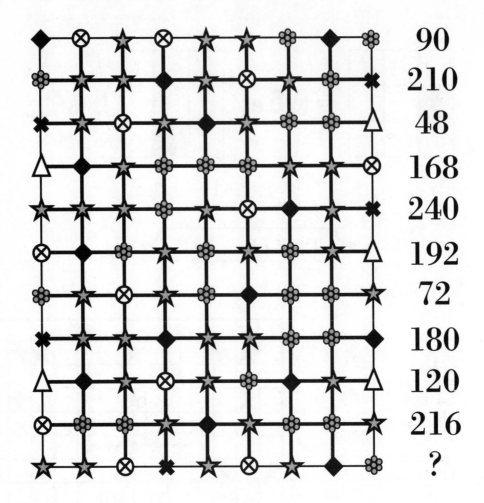

90
210
48
168
240
192
72
180
120
216
?

SEE ANSWER 168

Fill in the blank squares.

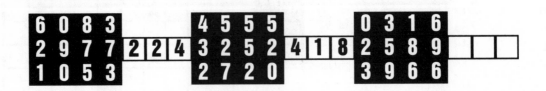

SEE ANSWER 184

PUZZLE 115

What is the missing number?

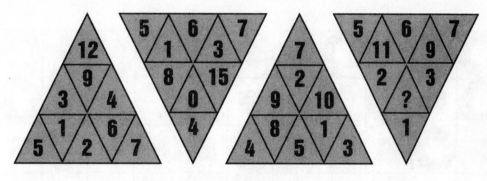

SEE ANSWER 112

PUZZLE 116

This system is balanced. How heavy is the black box (ignoring leverage effects)?

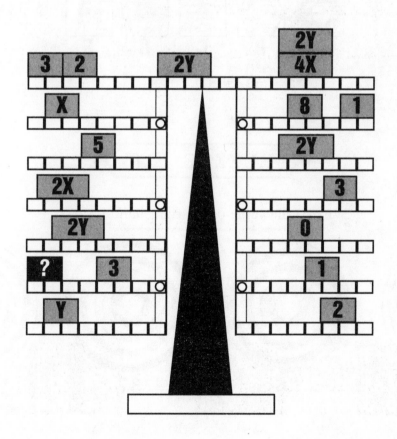

SEE ANSWER 140

63

PUZZLE 117

Each like shape has the same value.

Which shape should replace the question mark?

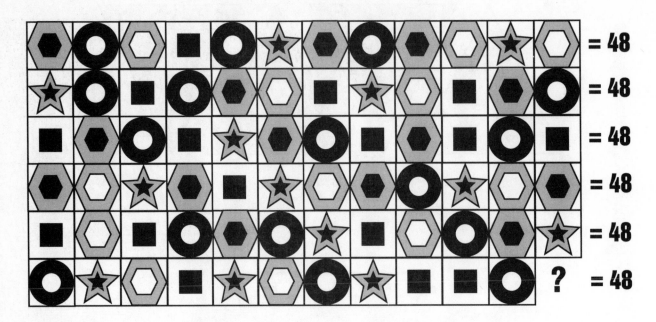

= 48
= 48
= 48
= 48
= 48
? = 48

A   B   C   D   E

SEE ANSWER 185

PUZZLE 118

What is the value of the right-hand target?

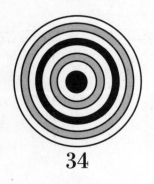   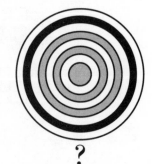

34   36   37   ?

SEE ANSWER 113

MISSION IMPROBABLE

The year is AD 2150. The situation is critical. Earth's protective shield has been penetrated by the pooch, a doglike race from the planet Remus in the Canis Major constellation. The aliens despise the human race as little more than fleas, and they intend to blast the earth apart for its mineral content. So they have implanted a bomb deep within the earth's core, timed for detonation in just a twelfth of the time it takes our planet to rotate on its axis. Having set the bomb, the pooch are off to investigate the rest of the planets in our solar system.

The bomb, put in place with teleporter technology, is impossible to defuse. The end is imminent and almost inevitable. The last and only hope for our planet is a teleport keyboard which the pooch left behind with a codebook, in the remote chance that there is, after all, some intelligent life on earth.

Survival Instructions

The keys are sensitized to receive your handwritten solutions to the following series of problems set by the pooch. If, for example, the answer to 1A is 5, write 5 on the key at 1A. Be careful – if you mark down the wrong solution to any problem, the bomb detonates, and the world explodes. Can you save the world? Don't mess this up – your fellow earthlings depend on you!

To find the solutions for row D, total the numbers you put in each column, and add the digits of the results to arrive at a single digit. For example, 25 becomes 2 + 5 = 7, and 59 becomes 5 + 9 = 14, 1 + 4 = 5. Once you have completed the D row, total all the D solutions together and again add digits of the results to arrive at a single digit. If you have found the correct solution to each of the 30 puzzles, you will find the figure which corresponds to the number of times the top left key must be pressed to send the bomb back to the pooch. If you cannot send the bomb home within the time limit, or if you press the button the wrong number of times, the earth is finished. To get the correct solution, you cannot afford to make any mistakes.

For those of you who accept defeat, all the answers to these puzzles are on page 80.

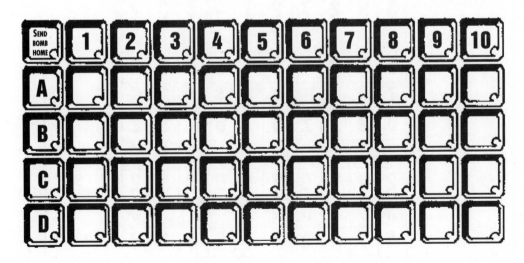

Hidden within the serial number on this soldier's helmet are two numbers that when multiplied together give 12186984. When you find the two numbers, add the digits of the lower one to get a single figure. This will give you the solution for the key 1A.

SEE ANSWER 6

PUZZLE 2

Discover the patterns that lie within this grid to find the missing numbers. The equal second lowest of those numbers is the solution for the key 1B.

A	B	C	D	E	F	G	H	I	J
3	9	2	7	2	1	4	8	3	2
2		1	2	3	0	6	7	4	2
3	8	2	4	4	1	6	5	3	0
7	3		1	4	0	4	7	2	8
8	9	7	2	9	1	8	4	3	2
1	8	0	8	3	2		5	2	0
2	9	1	8	7	5	6	2	1	2
5	3	1	5	5	2	5	8		0
4	1	0	4	3	1	2	9	1	8

SEE ANSWER 13

Find the value of the missing digit. Then subtract that value from the total of all the numbers and use the last digit of the resultant number to give you the solution for the key 1C.

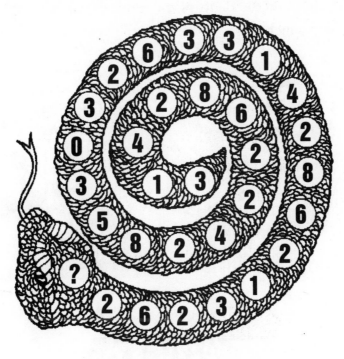

SEE ANSWER 18

PUZZLE 4

Zak is 6 earth years old. If Quark is three times as old as Zak was when Zak was a quarter as old as he is now, and Zak's brother is half the age of Quark's sister who is two-and-a-half times Quark's age, how old is Zak's brother in earth months? When you know the answer, divide it by three. The first number of this answer is the solution to 2A.

SEE ANSWER 25

Albert Einstein's pin has 190 on it, based on all the letters of his family name. Work out the logic of this and the number that should be on Harry S. Truman's pin. Multiply all the numbers on Truman's pin together, then add the digits of the result to reach a single figure which is the solution for the key 2B.

SEE ANSWER 30

PUZZLE 6

This system is in balance. How heavy is the black box?

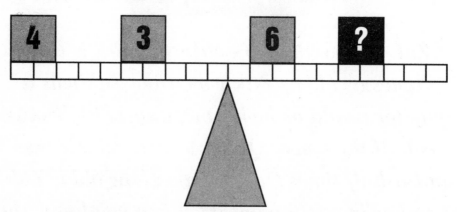

When you know the answer, subtract it from the square root of 36 and multiply the result by 2. The end product is the solution for the key 2C.

SEE ANSWER 23

Work out the missing value, then multiply the value of the rose by 3
and subtract the missing value from the result to give you the
solution for the key 3A. Each like shape has the same value
and no different shapes have the same value.

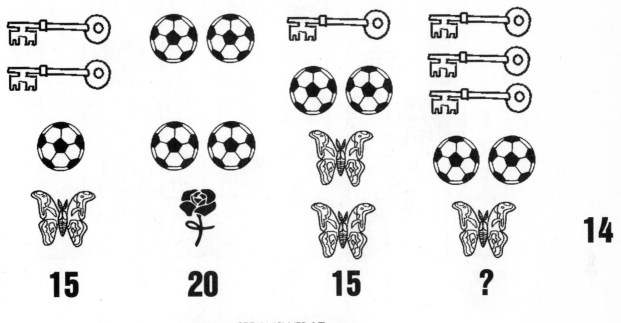

15   **20**   **15**   **?**   **14**

SEE ANSWER 17

It takes a Mark II Starfighter 30 minutes to travel between homebase and fighter station
Alpha, a distance of 6006 earth miles, flying into a 200 earth miles per hour headwind for the
first third of the journey, a 150 earth miles per hour headwind for the second third of the
journey, and a 100 earth miles per hour headwind for the last third of the journey.
Work out the average speed of the starfighter for the trip in earth miles per hour.
The middle number of that speed is the solution for the key 3B.

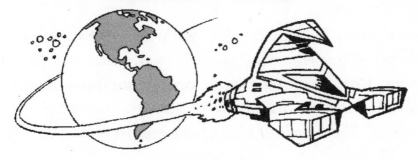

SEE ANSWER 5

PUZZLE 9

Here is a test of your ability to concentrate. Calculate the missing value and add the digits of the result to arrive at a single figure that is the solution for key 3C.

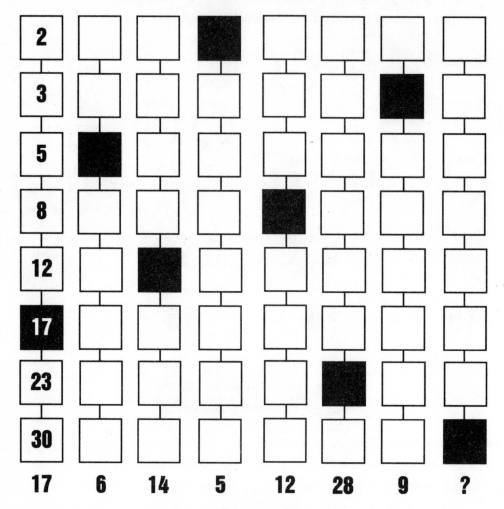

SEE ANSWER 12

PUZZLE 10

Jane collects Martian rocks. A third of her rocks are blue. A quarter of her rocks are white. The remaining 10 rocks are green. Work out how many rocks Jane has altogether and divide the right digit of the result by a quarter of the left digit. The result of that is the solution for the key 4A.

SEE ANSWER 29

PUZZLE 11

Pooch children can only recognize black and white, but they can do this problem easily. Insert the missing numbers under PINK, then use the right-hand digit of the value on the bottom-right quadrant to obtain the solution to the key 4B.

SEE ANSWER 22

PUZZLE 12

What number, when you add six and multiply the result by four, then add ten to that and subtract one tenth of the result, gives you a number that when divided by seven gives you nine? When you know the number, use it as the solution for key 4C.

SEE ANSWER 16

PUZZLE 13

Insert the missing numbers around the hexagon, in the same order as the first two examples, and subtract C from F. When you have done that, add the digits of the result to find the solution for key 5A.

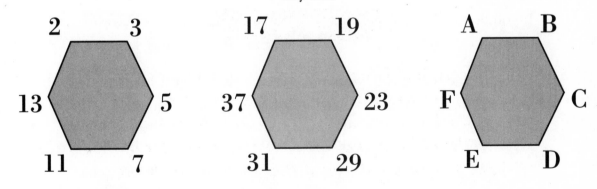

SEE ANSWER 4

PUZZLE 14

Prove that you have a capacity for pooch logic.
Decide which number grid, A, B, C D, E or F, is next in the logical
sequence, selecting from those in the box.

1 9 10 5 | 11 2 6 12 | 13 7 3 14 | 8 15 16 4

2 10 11 6 | 12 3 7 13 | 14 8 4 15 | 9 16 17 5

3 11 12 7 | 13 4 8 14 | 15 9 5 16 | 10 17 18 6

?

4 13 11 8 | 12 5 9 15 | 16 10 6 17 | 11 18 18 7
A

4 12 13 8 | 14 5 9 15 | 16 10 6 17 | 11 18 19 7
B

4 12 13 8 | 16 5 9 17 | 14 10 6 15 | 11 18 19 7
C

4 12 13 8 | 14 5 9 15 | 16 10 6 17 | 11 19 20 7
D

4 12 13 8 | 14 5 9 15 | 17 11 6 16 | 10 18 19 7
E

4 12 13 8 | 14 5 9 15 | 16 10 6 17 | 19 18 11 7
F

If you decide that it is A, your solution for key 5B is 1.

If you decide that it is D, your solution for key 5B is 4.

If you decide that it is B, your solution for key 5B is 2.

If you decide that it is E, your solution for key 5B is 5.

If you decide that it is C, your solution for key 5B is 3.

If you decide that it is F, your solution for key 5B is 6.

SEE ANSWER 11

Star A and star B lie on the corners of this box-shaped constellation. What is the direct distance from A to B? The answer is your solution for the key 5C.

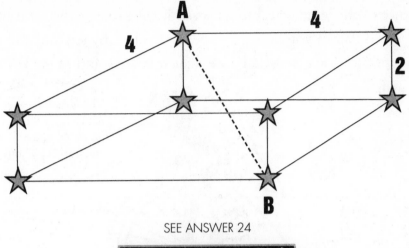

SEE ANSWER 24

Zed, leader of the Chicago Headchoppers, has foolishly forgotten part of the keycode to his hoverpad. If you can find the missing letter and number you will be able to subtract the digit from the alphanumeric value of the letter to find the solution for key 6A.

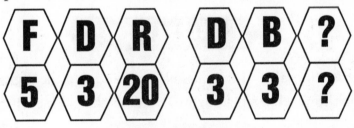

SEE ANSWER 28

Few species are capable of working out the logic of this triangular puzzle to find the missing number. If you can do it there is just a chance that you can help to save your planet. Use the missing number as the solution to key 6B.

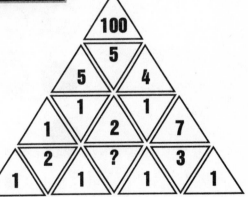

SEE ANSWER 21

Using the information on this diagram, work out the revolutions per minute (speed) of the small wheel, when the large wheel spins at the shown speed. The ratio of the circumference of the large wheel to its speed is the same as the ratio of the small wheel to its speed. When you know the speed, divide it by ten and add the digits of the result to reach a single figure, which is the solution for key 6C.

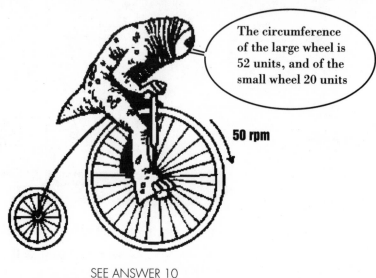

The circumference of the large wheel is 52 units, and of the small wheel 20 units

50 rpm

SEE ANSWER 10

PUZZLE 19

Calculate the value of the missing total and add the digits of the result to reach a single figure, which is the solution for 7A.

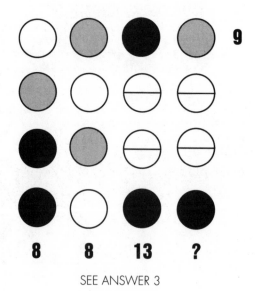

9

8   8   13   ?

SEE ANSWER 3

The most common digit in the answers to this crossnumber puzzle is the solution to key 7B.

ACROSS

1. The square that is less than 169 and more than 121
4. *13 across* + 10
5. *30 across* + 7
7. *32 across* + 301
8. *9 across* x *10 across*
9. Double the two digits immediately above
10. $\sqrt{1\ across}$ x 3
12. The next square number up from *10 across*
13. *11 down* – 40
14. A perfect square which would not fit here – 1
16. Last 2 digits of *30 across*
18. *10 across* ÷ 2
20. 4 consecutive ascending numbers
·23. *12 across* + *9 across*
24. The first two digits of *1 across* x 4
26. *31 across* + *18 across*
27. First and last digits of *32 across*
28. *27 across* ÷ 3, x 10
29. First digit of *13 down*, then *27 down* + 101
30. A perfect square greater than 100, but less than *1 across*

31. *9 across* x 4
32. 3 consecutive descending numbers

DOWN

2. *20 across* reversed – 192
3. *9 across* squared
4. Add *4 across* to the end of *10 across*
5. *1 across* – *9 across*
6. *13 down* + 91

11. *31 across* – 11
13. *9 across* x 100, + 1
14. *14 across* – 568
15. *14 down* – 117
17. *23 across* + 1900
19. *14 across* – 1477
21. *16 across* + 8
22. *4 across* x 100 – *31 across*
23. *15 down* – 2728
25. *27 down* – *26 across* + 2
27. 83 x any digit of *14 across*

SEE ANSWER 26

Four hairy xeeboks from the planet Scratch were each infected with the same number of itchers, but after being stopped by an interplanetary patrol of ten naive space cadets, a number of their itchers hopped onto the space cadets, so that they were evenly distributed between xeeboks and space cadets. What was the minimum number of itchers to have been on the xeeboks originally? When you know the answer, use it as the solution to the key 7C.

SEE ANSWER 15

Use the missing number from this grid as the solution for key 8A.

SEE ANSWER 9

PUZZLE 23

What length is the ladder (the dotted line) up to Zork's spaceship? When you know the answer add both digits together to get the solution for the key 8B.

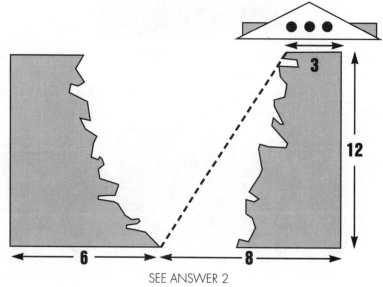

SEE ANSWER 2

Insert the missing number on this ancient symbol of elemental power from the pooch home-world, and use the number as the solution for key 8C.

SEE ANSWER 27

PUZZLE 25

How long in earth years, months, and days, did it take for a television transmission sent from the BBC in London, Earth, on the 26th September, 1952, to reach Remus, the home planet of the pooch, if the message was received there on the 21st of July, 1970? When you know the answer, add the digits of all parts of the result to reach a single figure which is solution for key 9A.

SEE ANSWER 20

PUZZLE 26

Find the missing number from this space cruiser, and use it as the solution to 9B.

SEE ANSWER 8

What weight is required on the left-hand side of this scale to keep the system in balance? Use the square root of twice that weight as the solution for key 9C.

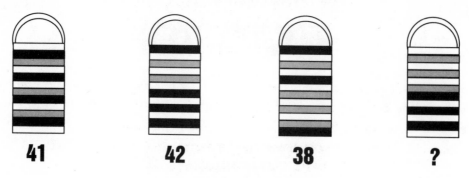

SEE ANSWER 1

One of the damper values is missing from these anti-G core piles. When you know the value, add the digits of the result to reach a single figure which is the solution for key 10A.

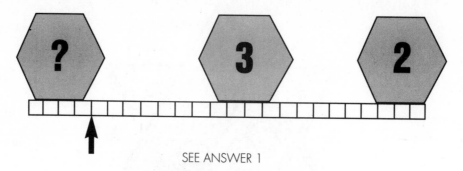

41   42   38   ?

SEE ANSWER 19

What is the missing value of these Zylon spaceships below? When you know the value, add the digits of the result to reach a single figure which is the solution for key 10C.

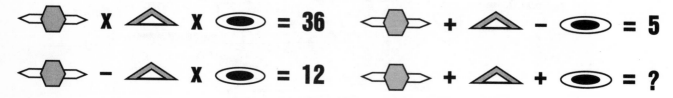

SEE ANSWER 14

Which of the surrounding sets of transporter cells fits into this logic system? If you think it is A, the solution for key 10B is 5. If you think it is B, the solution for key 10B is 6. If you think it is C, the solution for key 10B is 7. If you think it is D, the solution for key 10B is 8.

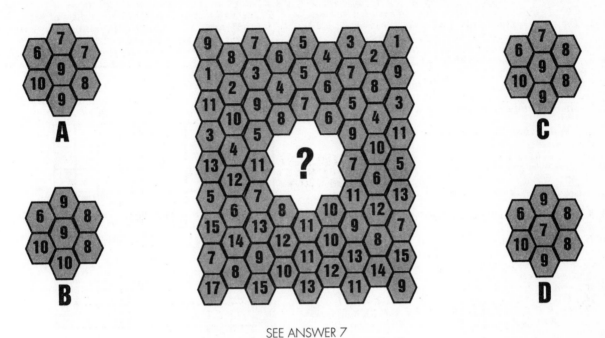

SEE ANSWER 7

But that is not yet the end of your troubles! Work out the code for the bomb teleport keyboard and send the bomb home before the earth explodes. Remember the consequences for delay or error!

1 8. The weight required is 32. $\sqrt{(2 \times 32)}$ = 8.

2 4. 8 – 3 = 5, so by using Pythagoras' Theorem, 5^2 (25) + 12^2 (144) = 169. $\sqrt{169}$ = 13. Thus the ladder is 13 units long. 1 + 3 = 4.

3 5. The missing total is 14. Shaded = 3; Black = 2; Split = 4½. 1 + 4 = 5.

4 5. These are the first 18 prime numbers, and they go in sequence from hexagon to hexagon. A = 41; B = 43; C = 47; D = 53; E = 59; F = 61. 61 – 47 = 14. 1 + 4 = 5.

5 0. The speed is 6006 ÷ 0.5 earth miles per hour = 12012 earth miles per hour. Wind speeds are irrelevant because both time and distance were given.

6 1. The two numbers are 9876 x 1234. 1+2+3+4 = 10. 1 + 0 = 1.

7 C (enter 7 on the keypad). The numbers run in sequence from right to left, and left to right.

8 7. Middle number reversed – top = bottom. 15700 – 9273 = 6427.

9 6. The first three numbers in each row, plus the last three numbers in each row equals, in succession, 999, 888, 777, 666, down to 111. 105 + 006 = 111.

10 4. The wheel spins at 130 rpm. Circumference of large wheel x speed in revolutions of large wheel ÷ circumference of small wheel (52 x 50 ÷ 20) = 130. 130 ÷ 10 = 13. 1 + 3 = 4.

11 B (enter 2 on the keypad). In each position, the number increases by 1.

12 1. The missing value is 37. 3 + 7 = 10. 1 + 0 = 1. The total of each column is found by adding successively 1, 2, 3, 4, 5, 6, 7, to each box total until a black box is reached. Boxes below the black boxes do not count.

13 4. In each row, column A x column B = columns CD; D x E = FG; G x H = IJ. The missing numbers are: col B = 6 (2 x 6 = 12), col C = 2 (7 x 3 = 21), col G = 4 (8 x 3 = 24 and 4 x 5 = 20), col I = 4 (5 x 8 = 40).

14 2. The missing value is 11. Left = 6; Middle = 2; Right = 3. 1 + 1 = 2.

15 7, giving 28 itchers. Distributed between 10 space cadets and 4 xeeboks, there would be 2 itchers each.

16 9. 9 + 6 (15) x 4 (60) + 10 (70) – 1/10 (7) = 63. 63 ÷ 7 = 9.

17 1. The rose is worth 8 and the other values are: Key = 5; Ball = 3; Butterfly = 2. The missing value is 23. Hence 3 x 8 (24) – 23 = 1.

18 4. Going from the middle of the spiral out 3 + 1 = 4, 4 x 2 = 8, 8 – 6 = 2, 2 + 2 = 4, 4 x 2 = 8, 8 – 5 = 3, 3 + 0 = 3, 3 x 2 = 6, 6 – 3 = 3, 3 + 1 = 4, 4 x 2 = 8, 8 – 6 = 2, 2 + 1 = 3, 3 x 2 = 6, 6 – 2 = 4. All the numbers added together = 108. 8 – 4 = 4.

19 3. The missing total is 39. Hence, 3 + 9 = 12, 1 + 2 = 3. Black bars = 5; White bars = 3; Shaded bars = 2.

20 6. The time required is 17 years, 9 months and 25 days. 1 + 7 + 9 + 2 + 5 = 24. 2 + 4 = 6.

21 2. Each row, multiplied together, equals the total of the row above added together. Thus, 1 x 2 x 1 x 2 x 1 x 3 x 1 = 12, the same total as the row above added, 1 + 1 + 2 + 1 + 7 = 12. Therefore, 1 x 1 x 2 x 1 x 7 = 14, 5 + 5 + 4 = 14 and 5 x 5 x 4 = 100.

22 7. Add 1 to the alphanumeric positions of each letter of the word PINK, and write the values in the order: bottom right (17), top left (10), bottom left (15), top right (12). The right digit of 17 is 7.

23 0. The left side weighs 48 units and the first weight on the right side weighs 12 units, so the unit 6 segments along must weigh 6 units. $\sqrt{36}$ – 6 = 0. 0 x 2 = 0.

24 6. 4^2 (16) + 4^2 (16) + 2^2 (4) = 6^2, hence the solution is = 6.

25 2. He is 67½ months (5⅝ years) old. 67½ ÷ 3 = 22½.

26 9 is the most common number (used 10 times).

[1]1	[2]4	[3]4		[4]3	9		[5]1	[6]2	8
	[7]1	0	6	6		[8]7	2	0	
	[9]2	0	[10]3	[11]6		[12]4	9		
[13]2	9		[14]9	9	9	[15]9		[16]2	[17]1
0			4			3			9
0			3			1			6
[18]1	[19]8		[20]1	[21]2	[22]3	4		[23]6	9
	[24]5	[25]6		[26]9	8		[27]7	5	
	[28]2	5	0		[29]2	8	4	8	
[30]1	2	1		[31]8	0		[32]7	6	5

27 6. The answer is 15. Multiply the numbers in consecutive points of the star and put the result between them. 5 x 15 = 75; 6 x 15 = 90. 1 + 5 = 6.

28 6. The missing letter is L. The missing number is 6. Give the letters their numerical value, then multiply diagonally to get the solution. 3 x 2 = 6 and 4 x 3 = 12. 12 – 6 = 6. L is the 12th letter.

29 8. There are 8 blue rocks, 6 white rocks, and 10 green rocks: a total of 24 rocks. (¼ of 2) ÷ 4 = 8.

30 1. Each letter in Einstein's surname is given double its alphanumeric value, and they are added together to give 190. President Truman's badge should say 174 (40 + 36 + 42 + 26 + 2 + 28). 1 x 7 x 4 = 28. 2 + 8 = 10. 1 + 0 = 1.

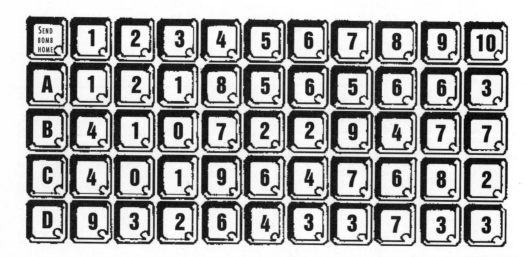

The sum of the 10 numbers in row D is 43. 4 + 3 = 7. Therefore, to save the Earth the Send bomb home button must be pressed 7 times.

An architect, after drawing plans for a room, finds that if he increases the length of the room by two units, and reduces the width by one unit, while maintaining the same height of ceiling, the room will have the same volume. If the difference between the original dimensions was three units, what were the length and breadth of the room on the original drawing?

SEE ANSWER 141

PUZZLE 120

Use three straight lines to divide this square into five separate sections containing a total of 52 in each.

```
7  3   7  0    4    3   6  1
   4      1       54    0
   4    0     2    0    2
 5    3   6     0    2    5
  1   5         9          1
 9              8    7     1
   2    9   5
 0  2       4   1  0   0
  7   0  1 9  7 3   3 1    7
                         1
      2    3      8  7   8
   3    0   5   3    2  0 4
      9    7   1       3
 6   0    2   1    3  6  3
```

SEE ANSWER 90

PUZZLE 121

In four moves of two pieces, make two numbers of alternating backgrounds, such that when you subtract one from the other, the result is 671. You must not finish with any gaps between the numbers but they will occur as you work through the puzzle.

SEE ANSWER 106

PUZZLE 122

What is the missing number?

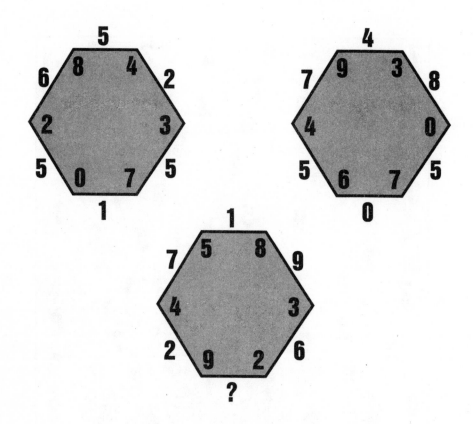

SEE ANSWER 127

Which two numbers below, when you put them together and
multiply the result by one of the other numbers, produces
12345678 as a result?

21 43 65 990 453 7765 8213 8890 6 5578 34 44
6012 05476 8653 9963 3257 45 75 25 2057 43567
7833 301 2134 248 54 79 92 12 38 22387 457 908
98 3245 1144 0980 356 76 91 111 88 2345 905 1121
42 5567 233 2355 8807 5467 890 20 994 1123 4356
7879 4567 67844 86743 54389 33 22 89 345665
052340 76435 345 120 243 94 123 100 53 400 335
555 613 1200 695443 2332 567 1023 845 77 325 205

SEE ANSWER 162

PUZZLE 124

The numbers in the three balls above each cell, when multiplied
together, minus the value of the numbers in the three balls below
each cell, when multiplied together, is equal to the value of the
numbers inside each cell. Insert the missing numbers.

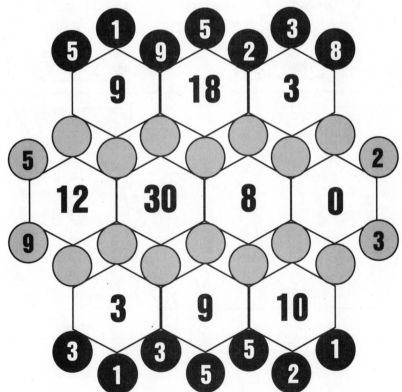

SEE ANSWER 169

PUZZLE 125

Insert the missing number.

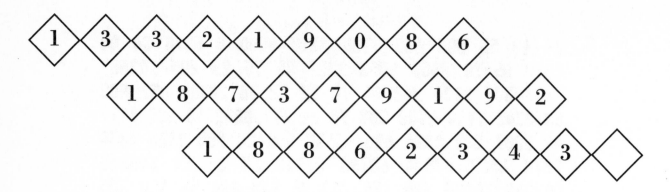

Row 1: 1 3 3 2 1 9 0 8 6

Row 2: 1 8 7 3 7 9 1 9 2

Row 3: 1 8 8 6 2 3 4 3 □

SEE ANSWER 148

PUZZLE 126

If each large ball weighs three units, what is the weight of each small black ball? A small white ball has a different weight from a small black ball. All small balls are solid; both the large balls are hollow.

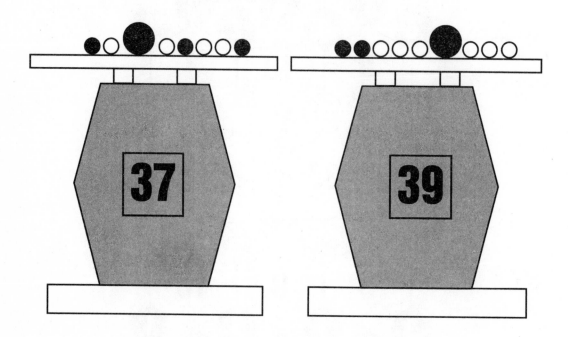

SEE ANSWER 124

Each like symbol has the same value. What number should replace the question mark?

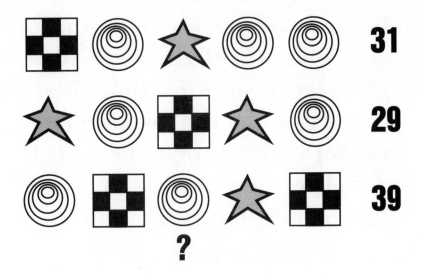

SEE ANSWER 170

Insert the missing value in the blank square.

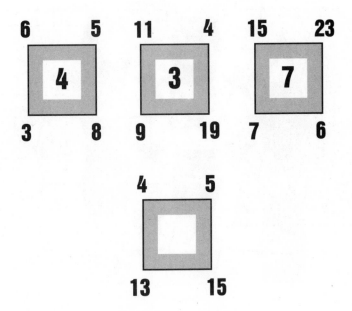

SEE ANSWER 149

Which two numbers, when multiplied together, give a result that, when added to itself, produces a number that, when the digits are added together, has a solution that gives the same result as the original two numbers added together and, if doubled, produces the same result as the original two numbers multiplied together?

SEE ANSWER 125

PUZZLE 130

What is the missing number?

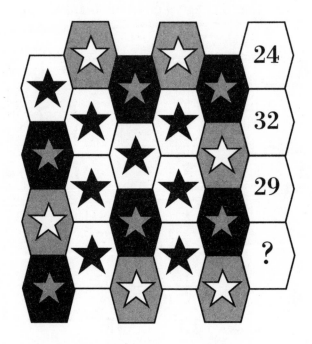

SEE ANSWER 186

Fill the numbers into the grid. They only fit one way.

ACROSS

69	263	726	1761670
76	328	751	4256701
84	338	758	4971467
97	447	778	5231937
092	450	821	6368906
096	472	847	6579804
101	517	930	6596817
122	627	957	7062502
131	650	974	7554403
147	660	0379304	8369591
167	692	1062387	9511198
171	697	1291762	9512209
178	706	1518117	9974515
239	711	1751171	

DOWN

069	298915	1028507	7057147
106	412961	1508171	7081701
352	497811	1970788	7097230
353	517268	2567039	7097429
379	576816	3374277	7121176
461	584605	3602976	7607138
513	709656	4298164	7632154
573	720412	4650786	7948137
590	797991	5247127	8076467
126959	862178	5364561	9912061
162717			

(grid contains: 8 4 7)

SEE ANSWER 114

Put a value from below into each triangle so that the total in each square gives a value that makes each row, column, and long diagonal add to 203.

6 8 29 9 27 30 13

7 3 29 14 15 8 3

2 19 11 12 39 0

40 1 7 11 2 9 2

34 13 10 8 12 20

19 36 5 4 5 18 40

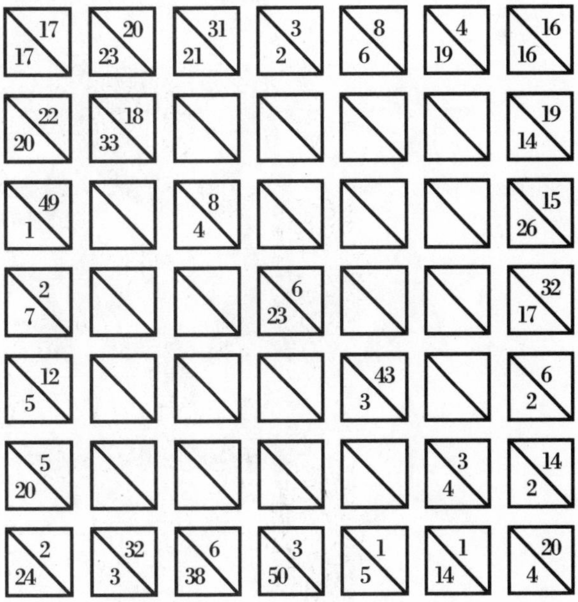

(grid of triangles with values:
Row 1: 17/17, 20/23, 31/21, 3/2, 8/6, 4/19, 16/16
Row 2: 22/20, 18/33, —, —, —, —, 19/14
Row 3: 49/1, —, 8/4, —, —, —, 15/26
Row 4: 2/7, —, —, 6/23, —, —, 32/17
Row 5: 12/5, —, —, —, 43/3, —, 6/2
Row 6: 5/20, —, —, —, —, 3/4, 14/2
Row 7: 2/24, 32/3, 6/38, 3/50, 1/5, 1/14, 20/4)

SEE ANSWER 142

PUZZLE 133

Insert the missing number in the blank square.

9	8
1	2

4	0
2	5

6	2
4	

5	5
4	9

8	2
3	4

7	1
2	3

SEE ANSWER 91

PUZZLE 134

What is the missing number?

SEE ANSWER 97

Express a half, using all the digits from one to nine.

SEE ANSWER 128

Decode the logic of the puzzle to find the missing number.

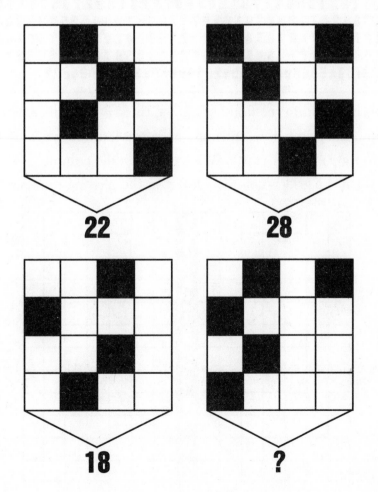

SEE ANSWER 163

What are the individual values of the black, white and shaded hexagons.

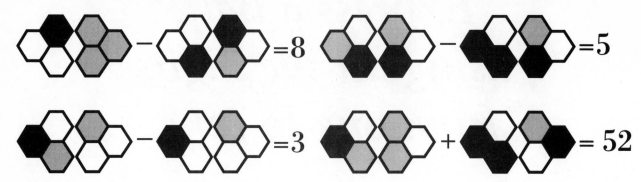

SEE ANSWER 98

1022493847460987123454668834712948876255455
4470112313501576120869252818027953987091 7
2935389201026039167071769815995650329003072
2918077807697853260892991202917077197830092
10325052516728962909609138507990985032910929
9107827364569708236554231098467392909046222

Somewhere within the number above, there is a number which, if
put into the grid below, starting at the top left and working from
left to right, row by row, will have the middle column as shown
when the grid is completed. Put in the missing numbers.

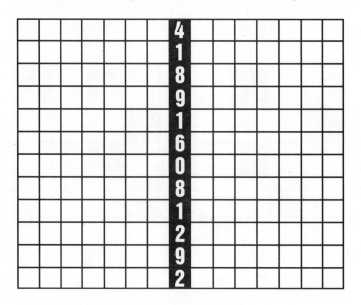

SEE ANSWER 129

Find within this number, a 6-digit number which, when divided by three gives a 5-digit palindromic number. (The number is the same reading from the left and the right.)

1 3 9 1 4 0 5 9 2 1

SEE ANSWER 164

The planet Spectra is widely known this side of the galaxy for its interesting inhabitants and large families. Zeebob and Gobop keep track of their family by classifying them according to certain physical characteristics, with most offspring belonging in more than one classification group. There are 18 offspring with green self-replicating fingers; 17 with three purple peppermint toes; 11 with red glowing eyes and blue hair; and 16 with luminous hypno-teeth of irresistible charm.

Looking at shared characteristics, 5 of those with three purple peppermint toes have red glowing eyes and blue hair; 5 of those with three purple peppermint toes have luminous hypno-teeth of irresistible charm, and 5 of those with three purple peppermint toes have green self-replicating fingers. Of those with red glowing eyes and blue hair, 5 have three purple peppermint toes, and 3 have luminous hypno-teeth of irresistible charm. Of those with luminous hypno-teeth of irresistible charm, 6 have green self-replicating fingers; 5 have three purple peppermint toes, and 3 have red glowing eyes and blue hair. Of those with green self-replicating fingers, 5 have three purple peppermint toes, and 6 have luminous hypno-teeth of irresistible charm. One member of the family can be classified under either green self-replicating fingers; three purple peppermint toes, or luminous hypno-teeth of irresistible charm. Two members of the family can be classified under either luminous hypno-teeth of irresistible charm; three purple peppermint toes, or red glowing eyes and blue hair.

How many offspring do Zeebob and Gobop have?

SEE ANSWER 171

Complete the analogy.

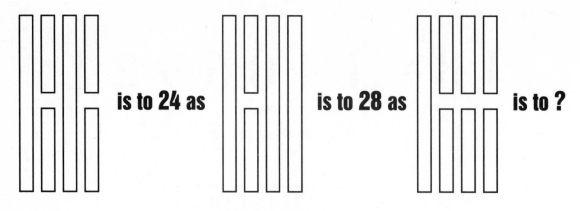

is to 24 as ... is to 28 as ... is to ?

SEE ANSWER 150

PUZZLE 142

Only the value of the positions of the black boxes in each column are added to give the number at the bottom (the numbers in the white boxes are a further clue). Work out the logic to find the value of the question mark.

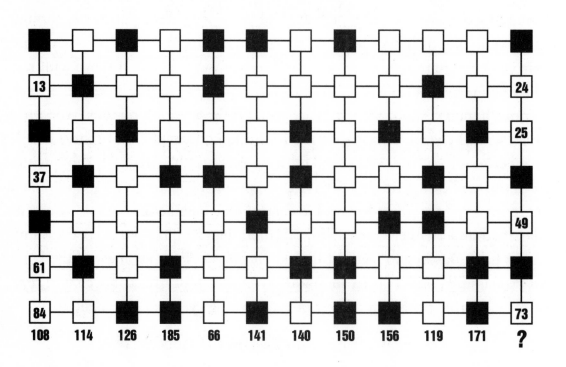

SEE ANSWER 126

PUZZLE 143

What is the missing number?

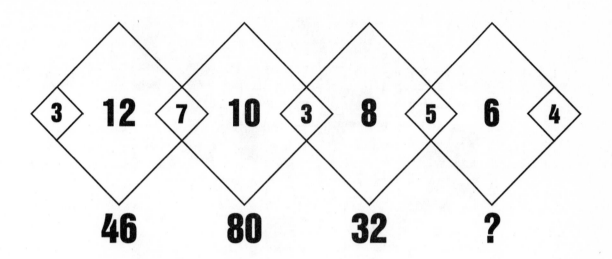

SEE ANSWER 177

PUZZLE 144

Which of these four sets is the odd one out?

1	9	0	3	3
0	3	3	1	9
	1		0	

4	2	8	1	1
8	1	1	4	2
	4		8	

3	0	9	2	2
9	2	2	3	0
	3		9	

2	4	3	5	5
5	5	2	4	3
	3		5	

3		9		3
9	0	3	3	1
3	3	1	9	0

A

1		2		1
2	8	1	1	4
1	1	4	2	8

B

2		0		2
0	9	2	2	3
2	2	3	0	9

C

4		5		2
5	2	4	3	5
3	5	5	2	4

D

SEE ANSWER 115

93

PUZZLE 145

Find a route from the top to the bottom of this puzzle that gives 175 as a total. Any number adjacent to a zero reduces your total to zero.

SEE ANSWER 143

PUZZLE 146

How many bacteria cultures should be in the Petri dish with the question mark?

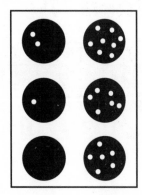
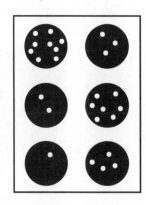
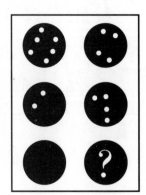

SEE ANSWER 92

PUZZLE 147

Insert the appropriate value in the blank triangle.

SEE ANSWER 116

PUZZLE 148

Which 2-digit number, the values of which when added together total 10, will always divide exactly into any 8-digit number in which the first four digits are repeated in the second half in the same order?

SEE ANSWER 144

If it takes twelve men two hours to dig a hole two feet long by two feet wide by two feet deep, how long will it take six men to dig a hole twice as long, wide and deep?

SEE ANSWER 93

PUZZLE 150

121938161	298561129	593734058	713213284
187828984	373954020	622992359	825861951
215442670	417262383	731874334	842522382
258901049	530289165	751287578	964582595
270127824	573762717	770017983	989893113

Locate the position of the numbers in the box above on the grid below. You may travel in any direction, but the lines have to be straight and no numbers are missed out.

```
5 5 9 3 3 1 2 1 7 9 8 5 2 7 9
5 2 1 7 3 8 5 1 2 8 5 3 5 0 6
1 7 1 8 1 4 3 9 5 6 0 1 0 5 0
2 0 3 8 9 2 8 7 1 4 2 9 2 0 7
6 1 9 7 1 5 3 9 3 8 4 5 3 6 2
5 2 7 3 6 2 8 1 7 9 8 2 4 9 0
1 7 2 1 8 2 1 5 2 9 5 3 6 0 7
5 8 1 9 0 3 7 9 0 7 3 4 2 7 5
4 2 7 3 9 8 2 1 3 4 5 1 0 7 0
9 4 5 8 7 2 0 6 7 8 3 0 7 2 2
4 3 9 0 2 4 3 8 2 4 1 7 5 1 0
0 8 1 5 9 8 1 5 6 7 9 6 3 8 7
9 5 3 4 7 3 9 2 9 4 1 8 1 9 7
0 2 5 1 7 5 1 8 3 0 5 4 0 3 5
8 1 0 3 8 1 3 0 4 1 3 6 1 7 6
```

SEE ANSWER 99

Find two numbers so that the
square of the first plus the second,
added to the square of the second
plus the first equals 238.

SEE ANSWER 130

PUZZLE 152

What is the missing number?

SEE ANSWER 165

Each like symbol has the same value.
Work out the value of the missing digit.

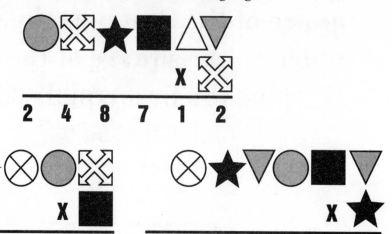

SEE ANSWER 172

PUZZLE 154

Which block of cells fits logically into the space?

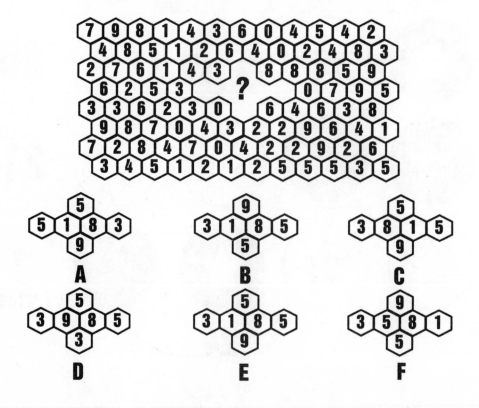

SEE ANSWER 151

A girl asks her mother's age and is told, "Six years ago I was nine times your age. Now I am only three times your age." What are the present ages of the girl and her mother?

SEE ANSWER 117

{ PUZZLE 156 }

How many revolutions per minute does the small wheel make?

? rev / minute

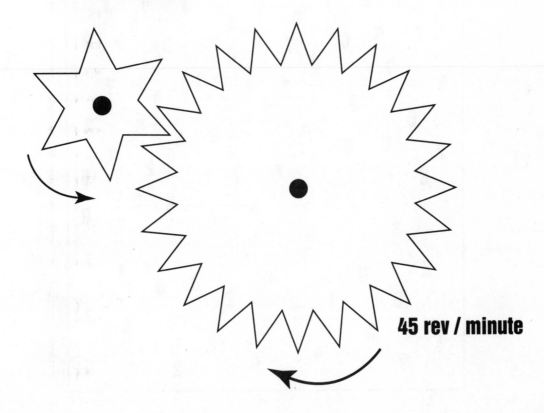

45 rev / minute

SEE ANSWER 178

PUZZLE 157

What is the missing point value?

SEE ANSWER 152

PUZZLE 158

Use three straight lines to divide this square into five sections, each
of which contains a total value of 60.

```
1   9   3   7       1       4   9   3
    7   9   8   0       3       3   5   9
        7       0   3       0
8           0           1       0   7
        5               1
    0   5       4           6   6   2
2               1   1   0   6       0
    8               7   7       2       9
            9           3       8   3
        3           4           7   0
                    9               7
            1                   1
2       0       4       3   6       7
    8       1       2       0   5   3
1       5                       2   9
    5           4   4       2   2   9
```

SEE ANSWER 94

100

PUZZLE 159

Use logic to find which shape has the greatest perimeter.

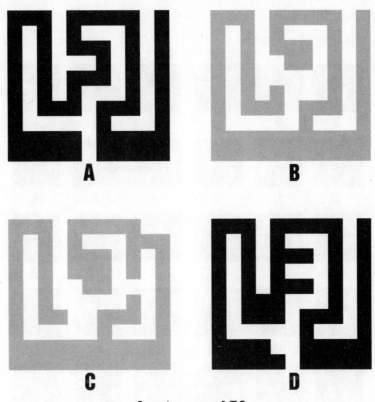

A   B

C   D

SEE ANSWER 179

PUZZLE 160

Supply both the missing numbers.

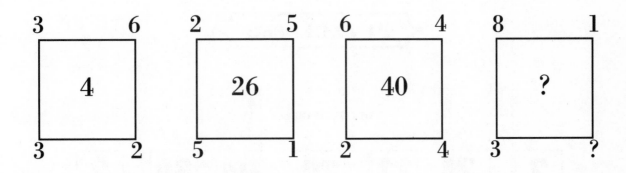

SEE ANSWER 107

101

PUZZLE 161

Find the block in each row which, when you multiply the highest two numbers together, and add the other two digits in the block to the product to arrive at a solution, then add the solutions from the chosen blocks in the other rows together, will give you the highest possible total. Repeat the process to also find the lowest possible total.

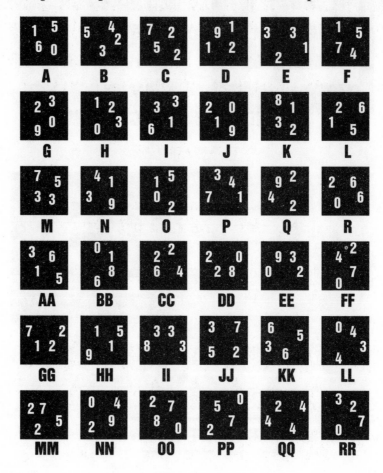

SEE ANSWER 145

PUZZLE 162

What number comes next in the sequence to replace the question mark?

2   7   11   20   38   69   ?

SEE ANSWER 118

What number, when you multiply it by three and multiply the result by seven and then add both of the resultant digits, and multiply the result of that by itself, when you add nineteen, gives a number that is a perfect square which can be divided exactly by only seven smaller numbers (excluding one), two of which are prime and two of which are perfect squares?

SEE ANSWER 100

PUZZLE 164

Find hidden within the stars, a long multiplication sum with a six-figure result.

SEE ANSWER 131

Make an exact quarter using all these numbers, and no other.

2 5 2 5 2 5 2 5 0

SEE ANSWER 166

The values represented by the black segments surrounding each number, are processed in two stages to get the numbers in the middle of each system. Find the missing number.

SEE ANSWER 173

Find the missing number.

8   2   3   1   8   4
9   2   3   2   0   ?

SEE ANSWER 157

PUZZLE 168

Which number replaces the question mark?

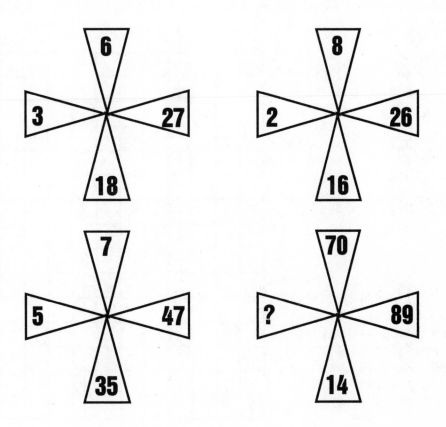

SEE ANSWER 132

What is the missing profit figure?

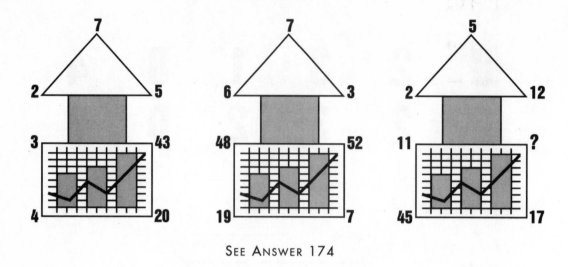

SEE ANSWER 174

Fill the numbers into the blank spaces. There is only one correct way.

ACROSS

30	326	649	2768259
74	359	659	4346540
87	386	691	5783968
93	390	697	6281307
018	467	721	6445535
042	496	735	6490916
133	516	918	6906308
148	519	929	7590936
273	563	954	9473460
298	619	989	9798259
306			

DOWN

043	928	2369674	7533652
192	165263	3268959	7934895
313	320469	4906736	9219367
333	372108	5176453	9452695
344	697469	5364749	9497059
460	0840396	6089148	9687097
521	0929969	7485571	9759968
863			

SEE ANSWER 153

Discover the vital relationship between all of these numbers to find the missing number.

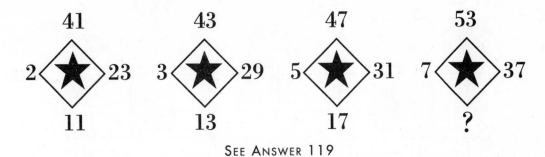

SEE ANSWER 119

What is the value of the target on the right?

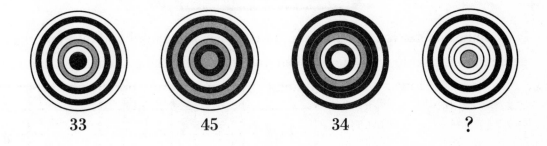

33   45   34   ?

SEE ANSWER 181

A perfect number is a number that is equal to the sum of its factors, excluding itself. The first is 6 (1 + 2 + 3). The next is 28 (1 + 2 + 4 + 7 + 14). The third perfect number falls somewhere between 350 and 550. What is it?

SEE ANSWER 180

PUZZLE 174

This system is balanced. How heavy is the black box (ignoring leverage effects)?

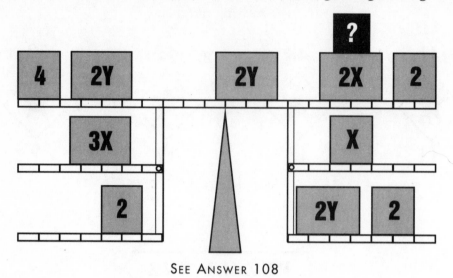

SEE ANSWER 108

PUZZLE 175

Put numbers in the squares above and below each diamond and multiply them together. Do the same with the numbers to the left and right of each diamond and subtract the lower result from the higher to obtain the middle numbers.

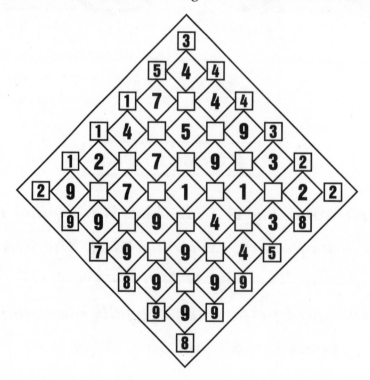

SEE ANSWER 146

If two is added to both the top and bottom of a certain fraction, its value becomes a half. If two is subtracted from both the top and bottom of that same fraction, its value becomes a third. What is the fraction?

SEE ANSWER 95

PUZZLE 177

What is the missing value of this logic series?

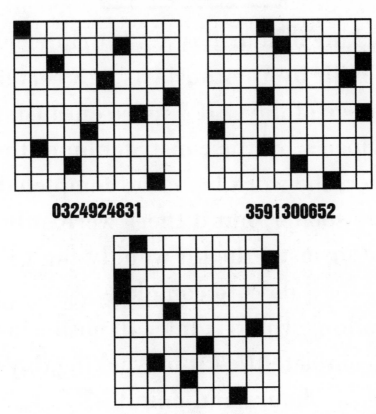

0324924831   3591300652

?

SEE ANSWER 101

Complete the analogy.

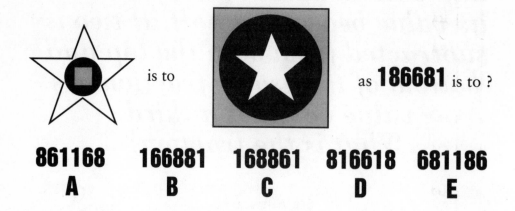

is to ... as **186681** is to ?

861168   **166881**   **168861**   **816618**   **681186**
A   B   C   D   E

SEE ANSWER 137

PUZZLE 179

Working 8-hour days, a kit glider can be built by 7 enthusiasts in a certain number of days. If 7 more enthusiasts helped with the construction of the glider, the work could be completed 7 days sooner, but if there were only 4 enthusiasts, the kit would take 24½ days to complete.

How long would it take 10 enthusiasts to complete the kit in working days, hours and minutes?

SEE ANSWER 96

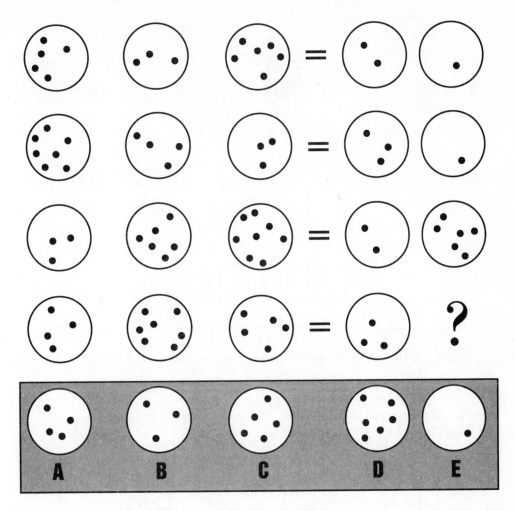

PUZZLE 180

Which Petri dish of bacteria cultures should replace the question mark?

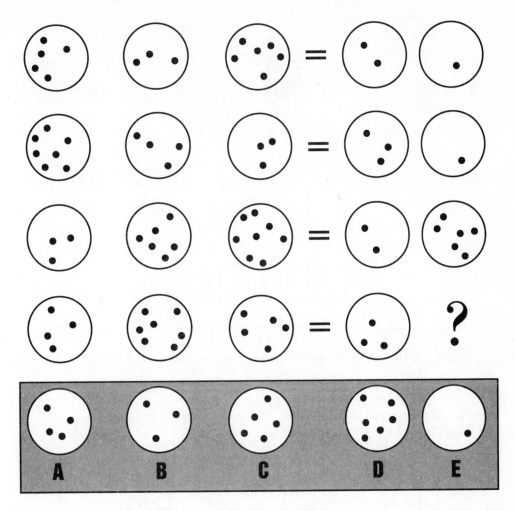

SEE ANSWER 102

PUZZLE 181

When you add two numbers their total is 101. When you compare the numbers, their difference is 27. What are the numbers?

SEE ANSWER 133

Insert the middle numbers.

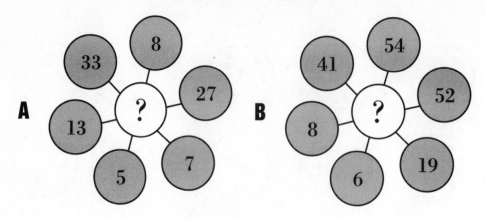

SEE ANSWER 158

PUZZLE 183

A rectangular plot of land is 28 paces shorter on one side than on the other. If the longer side were reduced by 34 paces, and the smaller side were lengthened by 40 paces, the area contained within the plot would be unchanged. What are the lengths of the sides?

SEE ANSWER 175

PUZZLE 184

What is the missing number in this sequence?

SEE ANSWER 154

PUZZLE 185

Insert the rows into the appropriate places in the grid to make all lines, columns, and long diagonals add to 105.

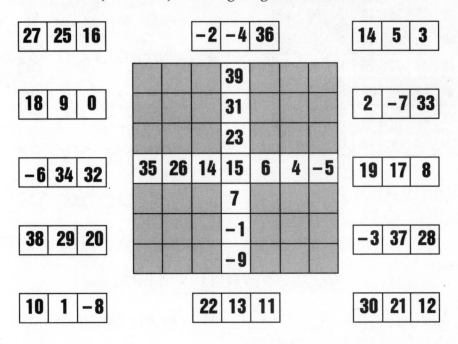

SEE ANSWER 120

PUZZLE 186

What weight balances the pulley system on the right?

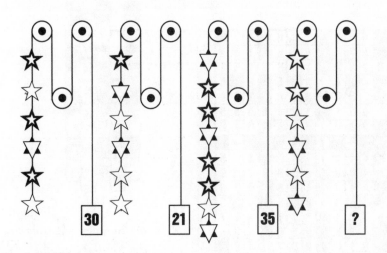

SEE ANSWER 109

ANSWERS

1

22	21	13	5	46	38	30
31	23	15	14	6	47	39
40	32	24	16	8	7	48
49	41	33	25	17	9	1
2	43	42	34	26	18	10
11	3	44	36	35	27	19
20	12	4	45	37	29	28

2 96. $4^2 = 16$; $16 \times 6 = 96$

3 32.
Diamond = 7
Circle = 4
Hexagon = 13
Square = 8

4 A. 54, B. 42. Opposite numbers are multiplied, divided, or added to get the numbers in the middle.

5 Thursday. 1952 was a leap year with 366 days. $366 \div 7$ (days in a week) = 52 remainder 2. Tuesday + 2 days = Thursday.

6 5 (4 big and 1 little).

7

8 78. Multiply opposite numbers and add the results to get the numbers in the middle. Thus 24 + 24 + 30 = 78.

9 200 Credits. $9 \times 25 - (4 \times 6.25) = 200$.

10

11 38 seconds after 8.43.

12 88. $88 + 880 + (4 \times 8) = 1000$.

13 18.
Elephant = 2
Walrus = 3
Camel = 4
Pig = 5

14 7162 and 3581.

15 Follow this route.

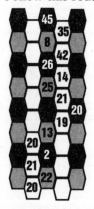

16 7. Take the middle number from the top left number. Multiply that by 2 to get the top right number. Add 5 to the top right number to get the bottom number.

17 D. The the binary numbers start at the top and work left to right, line by line.

1	1	0	1	1	1	0	0	1	0	1
1	1	0	1	1	1	1	0	0	0	1
0	0	1	1	0	1	0	1	0	1	1
1	1	0	0	1	1	0	1	1	1	1
0	1	1	1	1	1	0	0	0	0	1
0	0	0	1	1	0	0	1	0	1	0
0	1	1	1	0	1	0	0	1	0	1
0	1	1	0	1	1	0	1	0	1	1
1	1	1	0	0	0	1	1	0	0	1

18 20 July 1969. It was the date of the first manned lunar landing.

19 19. The top pair of numbers are multiplied together and added to the result of multiplying the bottom pair of numbers together. (2 x 8) + (3 x 1).

20 19. They denote the alphanumeric positions of numbers from 1 to 6. The first letter of six is "s", the 19th letter of the alphabet.

21

6	2	9	3	7
3	7	6	2	9
2	9	3	7	6
7	6	2	9	3
9	3	7	6	2

22 6. Add the value of the top two stars of each column to value of the middle two stars to get the value of the bottom two stars.

23 30 x 15 units (the pool's area becomes 18 x 25 units, or 450 square units).

24 2. The weight is positioned 8 units along, so it needs a weight of 2 units (8 x 2 = 16) to keep the system in balance.

25 9 minutes and 9 seconds after 1.

26 A.
Circle = 1
Diamond = 4
Square = 3
Triangle = 2
Hexagon = 5

27 7 people.

28 10.
Snowflake = 5
Candle = 3
Sun = 2

29 D. The paper would reach 3,355.4432 m, which is as high as a mountain.

30 C.
White = 7
Black = 5
Shaded = 3

31 7. There are 7 areas of intersection at this position.

32 28. Each row is a sequence of A + D = C, D + C = B and B + C = E.

33 25.
Circle = 4
Triangle = 8
Diamond = 5
Square = 2
The values are added when the shapes are combined.

34 10 m. The ratio of the flagpole to its shadow is the same as the ratio of the measuring stick to its shadow.

35 11954.
(45911 – 11954 = 33957)

36 3. There are two sequences in the series: 6 x 8 = 48, and 7 x 9 = 63.

37 46 points, taking this route:

9	4	5	3	6	1	8	2
8	1	2	2	3	2	5	1
6	9	9	1	2	4	3	5
4	8	1	3	5	2	6	1
1	4	3	7	6	3	1	4
9	2	4	8	6	4	5	3
4	2	9	4	8	6	7	1
2	8	1	6	5	9	0	1

38 27. The bottom two digits expressed as a number, subtracted from the top two digits, also expressed as a number. The difference is halved and the result is put in the middle. 78 – 24 = 54. 54 ÷ 2 = 27.

39 19.
Shaded = 9
Black = 5
White = 3

40 42. The bottom number goes next to the top one to make a two-digit number; the left and right do the same. Then subtract the second number from the first.
96 – 54 = 42.

41 6. The right weight is nine units across to balance the left three units across. 6 x 9 (54) balances 18 x 3 (54).

42 194. $(1 \times 5^3) + (2 \times 5^2) + (3 \times 5^1) + (4 \times 5^0)$.

43 103.5

44 A. 24. Opposite numbers are divided or added to give 24.
B. 3. Opposite numbers are multiplied or divided by 3.

45 12½ turns. For every unit that the rollers cover, the beam is pushed two units.

46 77 square units.

47 There are 5 cards missing, leaving 47 in the deck.

48 1. The number is an anagram of Mensa, with numbers substituted for the letters.

49 D. The least number of faces touching each other gives the greatest perimeter.

50 16.

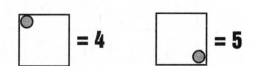

51 36.

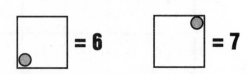

52

25 **49**
26 **10**
27
44 **28**
5 **29**

53 2. C = A − B, with the result reversed.
496324 − 235768 = 260556.

54 24. The pieces have the following values:

☆ = 5

☆ = 4

☆ = 3

55 E, G, G. These represent the numbers 577, which are added to the sum of the previous top and middle line, to get the bottom line.

56 0. The top two numbers are multiplied in shapes 1, 3 and 5. The answers are put as single-digit numbers in the top triangles of shapes 2, 4 and 6. In all the shapes the top two numbers are multiplied, then halved, 3 x 0 = 0.

57

58

59 2. The top four numbers, plus the number in the middle, equals the bottom four numbers. Hence 8765 + 567 = 9332.

60

6	8	0	9	4	1	**6**	4	1	6	2	2	2
3	4	5	6	3	4	**1**	2	1	9	1	8	3
6	2	1	6	1	4	**4**	4	3	2	7	0	8
9	2	2	8	4	6	**1**	5	2	9	5	5	0
0	1	6	2	1	9	**3**	2	0	0	0	2	5
2	8	1	2	1	2	**1**	5	8	5	8	7	1
9	3	9	4	5	0	**4**	6	3	9	5	1	2
3	1	6	1	7	6	**2**	1	1	3	2	6	7
7	9	2	2	8	9	**6**	5	6	1	2	3	1
0	2	2	3	8	4	**0**	4	6	1	2	8	9
8	5	4	0	4	3	**2**	6	1	6	1	4	2
5	2	6	1	6	0	**9**	3	4	1	7	2	8

61 Carlos is oldest; Maccio is youngest. (From oldest to youngest: Carlos, Juan, Za-za, Fifi, Jorjio, Maccio.)

62 12, 19, 26, 3, 10. The bottom line of a Magic Square, in which all rows, columns, and long diagonals equal 70.

63 72. It is the only non-square number.

64

3		5		4		4		3		3
	90		120		64		144		54	
2		3		2		2		6		1
	48		96		16		72		36	
1		8		2		2		3		2
	160		80		20		150		30	
4		5		1		5		5		1
	180		10		40		100		15	
9		1		2		4		1		3
	27		8		32		12		81	
3		1		4		1		3		9
	24		28		84		45		135	
8		1		7		3		5		1
	144		42		63		225		25	
3		6		1		3		5		1

65 24 ways. There are six alternatives with each suit at the left.

66 21 times.

67 15:03 (or 03.15 (pm) if the watch has the capacity to switch to 12-hour mode).

68 8 earth months. Zero has an orbit that takes $\sqrt{4^3}$ (8) times as long as Hot.

69 10 people.

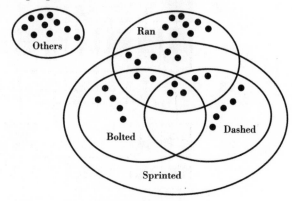

70 1. A + B = KL, C + D = MN, and so on.

71 A = 5. (a + b) − (d + e) = c
B = 0. (d + e) − (a + b) = c
C = 3. a + b + c − e = d
D = 2. c + d + e − a = b

72 Five men. Each man digs 1 hole in 5 hours, and thus 20 holes in 100 hours.

73 4. Start from the top left of the spiral and work in, successively subtracting and adding: 9 − 7 = 2, 2 + 5 = 7, etc.

74 22.
Rectangle = 8
Triangle = 3
Hexagon = 2

75 D. This is the only patch that works for all the lines.

12	21	30	−17	−8	1	10
20	29	−11	−9	0	9	11
28	−12				17	19

		−10	−1	8		
−13	−4	−2	7	16	18	27
		6	15	24		

−5	−3				26	−14
3	5	14	23	25	−15	−6
4	13	22	31	−16	−7	2

76 400. The numbers are the squares of 14 to 21 inclusive.

77 248. Long lines = 2, short lines = 1. Add the values on the right to arrive at the answer.

78 1258 x 6874.

79 B. Each nodule is given a value, depending on its position in the grid. The values are added together.

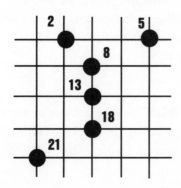

80 279. The numbers are added together and the sum + 1 is put in the next triangle. 106 + 172 = 278 + 1 + 279

81 B. The shaded spots represent the hands of a clock. 3:00 − 9:00 = 6:00.

82 25. Star = 9, Whorl = 5, Square = 3

83 34. Write the alphabet in a 3-row grid with the following values: A, J, S = 1; B, K, T = 2; C, L, U = 3; D, M, V = 4; E, N, W = 5; F, O, X = 6; G, P, Y = 7; H, Q, Z = 8; I, R = 9. Thus, Raphael = 9 + 1 + 7 + 8 + 1 + 5 + 3 = 34.

84 Any number. This amazing formula will always end up with the number you first thought of, with 00 at the end.

85 3. Add the spots and take the middle line from the top line.

86 3 units. The difference of 24 divided by 8.

87 P = 19. Map the alphabet into 2 rows of 13 each. Then add the numerical values of each row to get the value of the letters. A (1) + N (14) = 15. P comes two letters after N in the alphabet, so add two to the top and two to the bottom (16 + 3 = 19).

88 C. The 1st and 2nd numbers in each line, multiplied together, equal the last two numbers. The 3rd and 4th numbers multiplied together, equal the 6th and 7th. The 6th and 7th numbers minus the 8th and 9th numbers equal the 5th number of each line.

89 14. Divide the left number by 3 and add 4 to give the middle number. Repeat the sums with the middle number to get the right number. 78 ÷ 3 = 26; 26 + 4 = 30; 30 ÷ 3 = 10; 10 + 4 = 14.

90

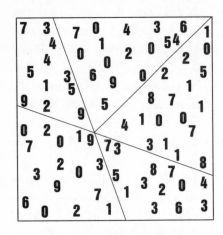

91 7. In each box, top left x bottom right = bottom left and top right. The products are a two-digit number reading up.

92 8. In each box the top two dishes expressed as numbers are multiplied to give the middle two dishes. The middle two dishes are then multiplied in the same way to give the bottom two. 6 x 4 = 24; 2 x 4 = 8.

93 32 hours. The hole will have eight times the volume. It would take 12 men eight times as long to dig it, and 16 times as long for 6 men.

94

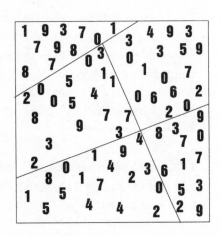

95 $$\frac{6}{14}$$

96 9 working days, 6 hours, 24 minutes. As it takes 4 enthusiasts 24.5 days (196 hours) to build the gilder, it would take 1 person 98 days (784 hours) and 10 people 9.8 days (78.4 hours) to complete the job. Each 0.1 of an hour is 6 minutes.

97 3. Reverse the second line and subtract it from the top line to get the bottom line. 43390 – 25587 = 17803.

98 Black hexagon = 2
White hexagon = 4
Shaded hexagon = 7

99

```
5 5 9 3 3 1 2 1 7 9 8 5 2 7 9
5 2 1 7 3 8 5 1 2 8 5 3 5 0 6
1 7 1 8 1 4 3 9 5 6 0 1 0 5 0
2 0 3 8 9 2 8 7 1 4 2 9 2 0 7
6 1 9 7 1 5 3 9 3 8 4 5 3 6 2
5 2 7 3 6 2 8 1 7 9 8 2 4 9 0
1 7 2 1 8 3 2 1 5 2 9 5 3 6 0 7
5 8 1 9 0 3 7 9 0 7 3 4 2 7 5
4 2 7 3 9 8 2 1 3 4 5 1 8 7 8
9 4 5 8 7 2 0 6 7 8 3 0 7 2 2
4 3 9 0 2 4 3 8 2 4 1 7 5 1 0
0 8 1 5 9 8 1 5 6 7 9 6 3 8 7
9 5 3 4 7 3 9 2 9 4 1 8 1 9 7
0 2 5 1 7 5 1 8 3 0 5 4 0 3 5
8 1 0 3 8 1 3 0 4 1 3 6 1 7 6
```

100 3. 3 x 3 [9] x 7 [63]; 6 + 3 [9] x 9 [81]; 81 + 19 = 100. 100 is 10^2 and it is divisible by 2 (prime number), 4 (also 2^2), 5 (prime number), 10, 20, 25 (also 5^2) and 50.

101 1009315742. The number of white boxes before the black box on each line, counting alternately from left and right.

102 B. Count the bacteria in each Petri dish, then multiply the first number by the second number and add the third number to the product. The 2-digit result follows. (4 x 7) + 5 = 33.

103 35. White hexagons have no value. Black hexagons are worth 1 in the top row, 2 in the second row, 3 in the third row, 4 in the fourth row, then 3 in the fifth row, 2 in the sixth row and 1 in the seventh row.

104 975310.

105 5. Each line contains three separate multiplication sums with the answer in between the multipliers. 10 ÷ 2 = 5.

106 The sum is 7153 – 6482 = 671. Move the pieces as follows:

```
1 2 3 4 5 6 7 8
6 7 1 2 3 4 5   8
6 7 1 2     5 3 4 8
6     2 7 1 5 3 4 8
6 4 8 2 7 1 5 3
```

107

```
8        1
   48
3        3
```

In each box, multiply the two bottom numbers and square the product to get the two top numbers. Read the top and bottom numbers as 2-digit figures and subtract the smaller from the larger. $\sqrt{81} = 9$; 9 ÷ 3 = 3; 81 – 33 = 48.

108 2 units.

109 24. Pieces have the following values:

☆ = 7

✡ = 1

☆ = 4

110 12345679 (x 63) = 777777777.

111 252.
Black triangle = 6
White triangle = 3
12 x 21 = 252.

112 5. The numbers in all the triangles add up to 49.

113 31.
White ring = 4
Black ring = 6
Shaded ring = 3

114

115 D. The two sections of each shape fit together to form a magic square. Each row of the other three add to 16, but each row of D adds to 19.

116 2. Each row adds to 40.

117 The girl is now 8, and her mother is 24.

118 127. Three adjoining numbers are added together in a continuous string. 20 + 38 + 69 = 127.

119 19. Map the prime numbers from 2 to 53 into four columns.

120

10	1	-8	39	30	21	12
2	-7	33	31	22	13	11
-6	34	32	23	14	5	3
35	26	14	15	6	4	-5
27	25	16	7	-2	-4	36
19	17	8	-1	-3	37	28
18	9	0	-9	38	29	20

121 456. The first symbols are worth 789; the middle symbols are worth 456; the right-hand symbols are worth 123.

122 $9(9^9)$ (nine [to the power of nine, to the power of nine]). Solve the top power first, giving nine to the power of 387420489. The result is a number so large that it has never been calculated.

123 8. The squares are numbered from 1 to 9, starting on the top left, from left to right, right to left, left to right.

124 Small black balls weigh 6 units. White balls weigh 4 units.

125 6 and 3. 6 x 3 = 18; 1 + 8 = 9 (and 6 + 3 = 9); 9 + 9 = 18.

126 121. Each block has a value according to its position in the grid. The blocks are numbered from 1 to 84, starting at the top right, and working right to left, left to right, right to left, etc. The black blocks in each column are then added together.

127 6. In each case, the sum of the numbers outside a hexagon equals the sum of the numbers inside it.

128

$$\frac{6729}{13458}$$

129

8	8	7	6	2	5	5	4	5	4	4	7	0	0	1
1	2	3	1	3	5	0	1	5	7	6	1	2	0	8
6	9	2	5	2	8	1	8	0	2	7	9	5	3	9
8	7	0	9	1	7	2	9	3	5	3	8	9	2	0
1	0	2	6	0	3	9	1	6	7	0	7	1	7	6
9	8	1	5	9	9	5	6	5	0	3	2	9	0	0
3	0	7	2	9	1	8	0	7	7	8	0	7	6	9
7	8	5	3	2	6	0	8	9	2	9	9	1	2	0
2	9	1	7	0	7	7	1	9	7	8	3	0	0	9
1	0	3	2	5	0	5	2	5	1	6	7	2	8	9
6	2	9	0	9	6	0	9	1	3	8	5	0	7	9
9	0	9	8	5	0	3	2	9	1	0	9	9	1	0

130 7 and 13. 7^2 (49) + 13 = 62. 7 + 13^2 (169) = 176. 62 + 176 = 238

131

132   5. The three smallest numbers are added together to give the largest number. The largest number is always on the right.
5 + 14 + 70 = 89.

133   37 and 64.

134

e	c	d	f	b	a	g
21	12	3	50	41	32	23
13	4	44	42	33	24	22
5	45	43	34	25	16	14
46	37	35	26	17	15	6
38	36	27	18	9	7	47
30	28	19	10	8	48	39
29	20	11	2	49	40	31
A	**B**	**C**	**D**	**E**	**F**	**G**

135

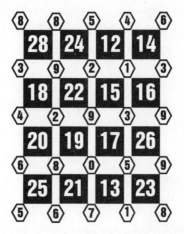

136

137   E. What was external becomes internal, and vice-versa.

138   16 people.

139   142857. The numbers are:
(x 1) 142857
(x 2) 285714
(x 3) 428571
(x 4) 571428
(x 5) 714285
(x 6) 857142

140 2 units. The difference of 16 divided by 8. The units to the right come to 104, to the left they are 86. 104 – 86 = 18. The blank box is 9 units across so 2 x 9 = 18.

141 It was 8 x 5 units. This becomes 10 x 4 units, retaining the area of 40 square units.

142

143 The route is:

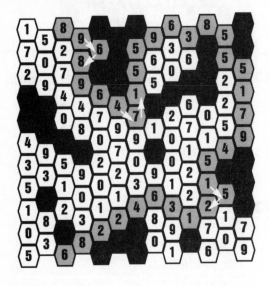

144 73.

145 The highest possible total is 268, using boxes F, L, M, BB, HH, OO. The sums are: (7 x 5) [35] + 4 + 1 = 40. (6 x 5) [30] + 2 + 1 = 33. (7 x 5) [35] + 3 + 3 = 41. (8 x 6) [48] + 1 + 0 = 49. (9 x 5) [45] + 1 + 1 = 47. (8 x 7) [56] + 2 + 0 = 58. 40 + 33 + 41 + 49 + 47 + 58 = 268.

The lowest possible total is 87, using boxes E, H, O, DD, GG, QQ. The sums are: (3 x 3) [9] + 2 + 1 = 12. (3 x 2) [6] + 1 + 0 = 7. (5 x 2) [10] + 1 + 0 = 11. (8 x 2) [16] + 2 + 0 = 18. (7 x 2) [14] + 2 + 1 = 17. (4 x 4) [16] + 4 + 2 = 22. 12 + 7 + 11 + 18 + 17 + 22 = 87.

146

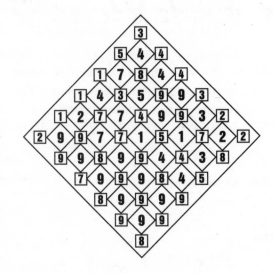

147 See opposite page

148 5. The first three digits expressed as a whole number, subtracted from the next three digits, expressed as a whole number, equals the last three digits. 623 – 188 = 435.

147

```
5 1 9 9 ★ 1 2 6 ★ 2 8 0 1
3 ★ ★ 9 3 2 ★ 4 2 1 ★ ★ 1
6 2 8 9 ★ 7 3 8 ★ 1 3 6 6
2 ★ 2 8 0 3 ★ 4 1 9 0 ★ 3
9 ★ 2 ★ 5 ★ 3 ★ ★ 0 ★ 5
3 4 8 5 ★ ★ ★ ★ ★ 4 2 2 7
★ 9 ★ 9 1 2 4 9 1 4 ★ 0 ★
1 2 3 3 4 ★ 1 ★ 5 3 8 0 2
★ 6 ★ 6 ★ 1 4 9 ★ 6 ★ 9 ★
5 6 1 8 2 ★ 3 ★ 1 2 3 0 4
★ 0 ★ 0 6 9 3 8 7 8 ★ 0 ★
9 ★ 5 ★ 1 ★ 8 1 ★ 6 ★ 5
8 6 4 ★ 1 2 3 4 5 ★ 1 1 8
1 ★ 2 3 4 5 ★ 2 1 3 3 ★ 6
9 7 8 3 ★ ★ ★ ★ ★ 9 2 7 7
2 ★ 2 ★ 2 ★ 1 ★ ★ 1 ★ 1
1 ★ 9 1 3 4 ★ 5 6 6 0 ★ 3
6 3 2 1 ★ 9 8 7 ★ 3 4 8 2
0 ★ ★ 7 6 9 ★ 8 2 3 ★ ★ 2
3 4 5 8 ★ 1 9 7 ★ 4 6 5 6
```

148   5. 623 – 188 = 435.

149   3. Add the left top and bottom numbers together, add the right top and bottom numbers together. Subtract the smaller from the larger to get the middle number. (15 + 5) – (13 + 4) = 3.

150   20.
Long bar = 8
Short bar = 2

151   E. Label each row of cells from the left, and do the following multiplications:
b x k = fg; c x j = eh; a x l = di.

152   1. The sum of the four smallest values equals the largest value. The largest value rotates by one turn clockwise each star.

153

```
⊕ 3 0 ⊕ 9 8 9 ⊕ 5 1 6 ⊕ 7 4 ⊕
1 4 8 ⊕ 4 6 7 ⊕ 3 9 0 ⊕ 5 6 3
6 4 4 5 5 3 5 ⊕ 6 2 8 1 3 0 7
5 ⊕ 0 ⊕ 2 ⊕ 9 5 4 ⊕ 9 ⊕ 3 ⊕ 2
2 7 3 ⊕ 6 5 9 ⊕ 7 2 1 ⊕ 6 9 1
6 4 9 0 9 1 6 ⊕ 4 3 4 6 5 4 0
3 8 6 ⊕ 5 7 8 3 9 6 8 ⊕ 2 9 8
⊕ 5 ⊕ ⊕ 6 3 ⊕ 3 9 ⊕ ⊕ 7 ⊕
3 5 9 ⊕ 9 4 7 3 4 6 0 ⊕ 3 0 6
2 7 6 8 2 5 9 ⊕ 9 7 9 8 2 5 9
0 1 8 ⊕ 1 3 3 ⊕ 0 4 2 ⊕ 6 9 7
4 ⊕ 7 ⊕ 9 ⊕ 4 9 6 ⊕ 9 ⊕ 8 ⊕ 4
6 9 0 6 3 0 8 ⊕ 7 5 9 0 9 3 6
9 2 9 ⊕ 6 4 9 ⊕ 3 2 6 ⊕ 5 1 9
⊕ 8 7 ⊕ 7 3 5 ⊕ 6 1 9 ⊕ 9 3 ⊕
```

154   6. The numbers in the left triangles of each pair of split blocks, when multiplied together, equals the numbers in the right-hand triangles of each pair of split blocks. 7 x 8 = 56.

155   Dog = 12
Horse = 9
Cat = 7
Pig = 5

156

Move one place to the right in the alphabet. A = 2, B = 3. The numbers to make espresso are E = 6, S = 20, P = 17, R = 19 and O = 16.

157   7. Each line is a multiplication sum without symbols or spaces.
8 x 23 = 184
9 x 23 = 207

158   A = 40, B = 60. Opposite numbers are multiplied or added to get the numbers in the middle.

159 24.
Elephant = 4
Pig = 2
Camel = 6

160 27. The left number is one-third of the top and the right is subtracted from the top number to give the bottom.

161 17 x 65359477124183 = 1111111111111111.

162 2057, joined by 613, x 6.
The sum is 2057613 x 6 = 12345678.

163 20. In each shape, the values are of the black squares. In column 1, they are worth 2; in column 2, they are worth 4; in column 3, they are worth 6 and in column 4, they are worth 8. The values are added together and the total goes at the bottom.

164 140592. 140592 ÷ 3 = 46864.

165 23. The shapes have the following values:

7 **9** **5** **2**

166

$$\frac{5555}{22220}$$

167 4. In each row, the numbers in the two left balloons equal the numbers in the three right balloons.

168 70. Each star is valued from 1 to 9, depending on its position in the columns from the left of each row. The values are then multiplied. The stars appear in columns 1, 2, 5 and 7, so the sums are:
1 x 2 (2) x 5 (10) x 7 = 70.

169

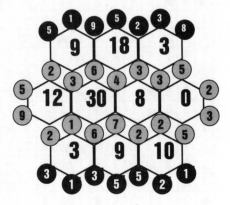

170 21.
Whorl = 5
Checkered box = 13
Star = 3

171 41 offspring.

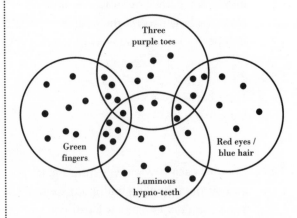

172 4. The sums are
124356 x 2 = 248712
248712 x 3 = 746136
746136 x 4 = 2984544
The shapes have the values above right:

172

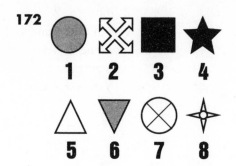

173 5. Use the values represented by the black spots in the puzzle, numbered as below. Multiply each top pair of values together to get the values for the bottom pair, and subtract the bottom left value from the top right value.
4 x 7 = 28; 7 – 2 = 5.

174 47. Add together all the numbers around each graph, bottom. Multiply together the three numbers around the roof, top. The answers should be the same.
5 x 2 x 12 = 120. 47 + 45 + 17 + 11 = 120.

175 68 x 40 paces (becoming 34 x 80 paces). The area remains 2720 paces^2.

176 100. The numbers inside each triangle total 200.

177 39. Each diamond contains three numbers. To get the bottom number, multiply the left by the middle, and add the product to the sum of the right and the left. (5 x 6) + 5 + 4 = 39.

178 180 revolutions. (45 revolutions x 24 teeth of big wheel [1080 movements]) ÷ 6 (teeth of small wheel) = 180.

179 A. The thinnest shape to cover an area always has the greatest perimeter.

180 496. 1 + 2 + 4 + 8 + 16 + 31 + 62 + 124 + 248 = 496.

181 32.
White ring = 3
Shaded ring = 9
Black ring = 4

182 + 29, x 7, – 94, x 4 and – 435. The sum is:
29 x 7 (203) – 94 (109) x 4 (436) – 435 = 1.

183 30. Multiply the top two numbers together and the bottom two numbers together. Then subtract the lower from the higher and then put answer in the middle. This is done continuously.
(12 x 7) [84] – (9 x 6) [54] = 30.

184 425. Reverse the top line, subtract the second line from that, and subtract the result from the bottom line to get the three figure sum for the blanks.
6130 – 2589 = 3541; 3966 – 3541 = 425.

185 B. The values of the shapes are:

 = 5

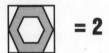 = 2

 = 6

 = 4

 = 3

186 27.

Shaded hexagon / white star = 3
Black hexagon / shaded star = 5
White hexagon / black star = 8